GOD IN MY HEAD

The True Story of an ex-Christian who accidentally met God.

Joshua Steven Grisetti

For you.

CONTENTS

"All great truths begin as blasphemies."

– George Bernard Shaw

ACKNOWLEDGMENTS

In a very direct way I must thank Becky Brown, a dear friend of my parents who gave me her copy of Todd Burpo's book *Heaven Is For Real*, which inspired me to write my own story. Perhaps she knew that over the years I had become increasingly skeptical of some of Christianity's teachings, and thought Burpo's book would help warm my heart back towards the faith. It was a sweet, loving gesture that I cherish.

In a less direct way, I must also thank my Southern Baptist parents, whose stalwart conservative upbringing provided the foundation upon which everything in the pages to follow was undoubtedly built. Not only they, but also the entire Christian community from my rural hometown in Virginia. I may not have turned out the way any of you had hoped, but I certainly enjoyed the ride, and I treasure the memories and morals that you all helped to instill.

In an even less direct way, I would like to thank all of the skeptics and cynics, Atheists, Agnostics, Unitarians, Jews, Christian Scientists, Mormons, Buddhists and other religious or nonreligious persons I've stumbled into conversations with throughout the years. A tiny piece of each of you is lurking somewhere deep in my subconscious, and therefore peppered throughout this odd memoir.

A few key hands helped shape the pages of this document into a presentable form. They are Erika Henningsen, Jon Paul Lindsay and Samia Mounts. Thank you, lads and lassies, for lending me your eyes, minds, hearts and spirits.

Lastly, I'd like to acknowledge my wise and beautiful ex-wife, Candice, whose disbelief fueled so much of my desire to better understand myself and the ridiculous world around me. She also directly inspired me to write this book so that I might, in her words, "finally shut up about it."

JOSHUA STEVEN GRISETTI

DISCLAIMERS WORTH DISCLAIMING

Firstly, my story involves a reckless misuse of multiple prescription and nonprescription drugs in combinations that are *potentially lethal*. This book is in no way a means of glorifying or condoning my irresponsible actions, and must not be confused for a recommendation of any kind. In that vein, any health-related information presented or implied within this book is purely anecdotal. I, the author, assume no liability for any damages or injuries that may result from the use or interpretation of any information within this book.

Secondly, this book is primarily about my unexpected encounter with God. However, in order to explain the experience fully, I must start at the very beginning. The first several chapters of this book are dedicated to explaining how my meeting with the Almighty came to pass.

To be sure, this is a true story, a spiritual memoir of sorts. Everything presented here is as truthful a representation of the actual events as can possibly be recalled from memory. I have, however, assigned fictional names and locations to the real-world people and places described in this book, merely to protect the anonymity of all involved.

Regarding the formatting of the chapters relating directly to my experience with God, the words that He spoke to me have been recalled from memory. While certain phrases are no doubt verbatim, I am inevitably paraphrasing most of what He said. This is self-evident, but given the subject matter I feel a strange compulsion to reiterate it. (There is something inherently uncomfortable about paraphrasing <u>God</u>, whether you believe in Him or not.) Also, the encounter seemed to span many years, and rambled non-linearly in all directions. It felt as if God unloaded a mountain of books in front of me and called it a "library." I, the "librarian" in this analogy, tasked myself to cataloguing all of that information, organizing it into a linear form in order to write it down. I don't suspect that my reformatting has distorted the message in any way, however I prefer to err on the side of complete transparency, so I'm mentioning it.

I'd also like to acknowledge that using personal pronouns like "He" and "Him" for God is an admitted misnomer. He specifically said that He was gender-neutral, but it is somehow easier to identify Him in the masculine sense. Perhaps this is because of the traditional male-centric view of God, "the Father." Nonetheless, if it bothers you in the slightest, feel free to substitute whatever vocabulary you like – He, She or It will do just fine.

Lastly, no matter what creed or walk of life you subscribe to, some of the ideas presented here will naturally appeal to you, while others repel you. I'm not necessarily making a case for or against any particular doctrine or point of view in the pages that follow; I'm simply trying to tell you what I saw and what I was told. Whatever positions you ultimately take on these matters, don't shoot the messenger. Follow your own divine instincts, and take *my* divine instincts with a grain of salt. Though I am happy to share them with you, they may or may not be compatible with your own. As the old saying goes: one man's trash is another man's spiritual awakening. Or something like that.

PREFACE

This book began as a kind of response to a book published in 2010 by Todd Burpo called *Heaven Is For Real*[1]. In that book, the author chronicles the trial of his three-year-old son Colton as he narrowly averts death after a ruptured appendix. Thankfully, Colton survived. Over the months and years that followed, Colton's parents learned that the boy had undergone an out-of-body experience during the emergency surgery that saved his life.

The author, Colton's father, claims that his son saw the doctors and nurses working on him, as well as his mother and father crying in separate rooms during the surgery. He then went to Heaven, where he saw Jesus dressed in white robes with a purple sash. He even sat on Jesus's lap and talked to him! He met John the Baptist, a choir of singing angels and a grandfather who had died 30 years prior to Colton's birth.

After the surgery, Colton allegedly became somewhat preoccupied with funerals, asking his parents to identify whether or not recently deceased persons were Christians. When his parents asked him why he wanted to know, he explained that Jesus had told him that only Christians (people who truly loved Jesus as their savior) could enter Heaven. All of this despite the fact that his parents swore they never taught Colton such doctrines prior to his near-death experience. Clearly, this proves that Heaven is "for real"!

Well, that's certainly one way to look at it. In fact, I find it to be an uplifting and perfectly normal way to view the world. Throngs of other Americans clearly agreed; the book hit #1 on *The New York Times* best-selling paperback nonfiction list in January 2011, selling over a million copies by April 2012.[2] This is impressive from a commercial standpoint, if not from a spiritual one.

Naturally, I realize that most people tend to expose themselves only to material that affirms their own preexisting beliefs, rather than complicate things with conflicting ideas. Christians are certainly not exempt from this phenomenon; in fact, in my experience, they are often the guiltiest culprits. Todd Burpo's book is a shining example; it became one of the highest selling books in the history of the genre, likely because it confirmed every iota of traditional, protestant Christian doctrine.

I would have been amazed if tribesmen in Africa had raised a three-year-old boy who then had a vivid hallucination about meeting Jesus Christ surrounded by singing angels. I might have even been intrigued if the boy had been the child of Atheists, then awoke from surgery evangelizing the Good News of Christianity. However, Colton was not raised by tribesmen, nor by Atheists. His father (who, not inconsequentially, wrote the book) was none other than a Protestant Christian minister from Nebraska.

Is it any wonder that Colton saw "Jesus" as a European-looking white man with long brown hair and green eyes, who wore a white robe with a purple sash? This image feels pulled straight out of the pages of a children's picture Bible. We have to presume that if Jesus actually appeared to Colton supernaturally, that he took a physical form similar to Colton's toddler-like concept of who Jesus was. That is, a comfortable fulfillment of a white, American three-year-old boy's preexisting notion of what "Jesus" ought to look like. If that is so, we're acknowledging that what the child saw *was conditioned* by his environment, which leads me to wonder how much of the rest of his vision was simply psychological conditioning.

To be fair, these are only the same questions I've asked of myself regarding my similar encounters with God and the afterlife. I believe it is a valid question for anyone who has had such experiences. By calling attention to these psychological links, I might be perceived as coldly dismissing people's intimate near-death experiences, however, as demonstrated by my own forthcoming testimony, I believe the truth may be far more complicated than that.

To be clear, I am not so cynical as to write an entire book pooh-poohing the theological or psychological implications of a child's spiritual journey, nor the enthusiasm of his parents. I do, however, wish to propose an alternative perspective on these kinds of experiences. Unlike Mr. Burpo, who offers his son's hallucinations under anesthesia as literal "proof" of God and the afterlife, I freely admit that what I am about to share with you is purely subjective. The vision of the God that I encountered was meant for me and me alone. I offer it to you not as proof of anything, but as a potentially new way of perceiving God's apparent interactions with mankind. My journey is merely a counterpoint example of how traumatic medical situations can affect the complex human brain in a variety of different ways. Or, to put it in religious terms, one might say "how the Lord works in mysterious ways."

If you haven't read *Heaven Is For Real*, fear not. It is not a prerequisite for reading this book, by any means. In fact, this will be my only mention of Burpo's book until the final chapter.

PROLOGUE:
JOURNEY ENDED, JOURNEY BEGUN

The window facing the parking lot was bright with midday sun. From inside, you might have mistaken the radiance for a warm summer's day, save the leafless trees that lumbered gloomily around the edges of the pavement. A cold wind off the East River always blew across New York City's Upper East Side this time of March, relentlessly rushing into the city from every break in the skyline. Today was no different.

The bare branches of the trees groaned quietly in the bitter air. Despite the pleasant sunbeams streaming into the room, my bones knew the apparent warmth was a lie – a mirage of a summer day that would not come for months ahead. I shivered, slightly, as if there were a draft, although I'm almost certain there was not.

A moment ago, none of this mattered. A moment ago, mere seconds past, I was not in New York. It was neither winter nor spring, day nor night. A moment ago I was neither alive nor dead.

I laid nearly flat as the machine tilted my body upright. Muffled rumblings began to coalesce into something familiar. Voices. Casual banter, the occasional laugh. The chatter seemed to be echoing through me. Slowly, my mind began to focus.

"The sun," I thought. "The branches. Winter. Nurses, Doctors, New York... I'm back! Just like He said I would be."

I began to laugh, weakly.

I turned to my left to find a middle-aged Jamaican woman staring

1

at me with wide eyes, her nose and mouth covered by a surgical mask. She jolted and let out the smallest gasp, suddenly frozen. It was as if she had come face to face with a ghost. In that brief moment, for all I knew, maybe she had.

My fatigued laughter must have been disarming enough to release some of the tension. Even though I could see only a small portion of her face above the mask, I noticed her eyes relaxing and her cheeks rising as if beginning to smile. She spoke, a short melodic sequence of words that I couldn't quite make out.

I quietly stared at her, trying to focus harder.

"Are you okay?" She asked again. Her smile seemed to drop slightly.

It was then that I realized I had her right hand in a death-grip. I'm not sure when I had grabbed it, but contextually I made the assumption that it was about the time she gasped and began staring at me as if I might have been a serial killer.

"I'm fine!" My voice boomed across the tiny room.

In my haste to appear remotely normal, I hit the gas a little too hard and overshot the volume mark on what might be considered appropriate indoor conversation. I felt sort of like an ogre who had just been taught to speak. Despite all the mystical revelations I had just witnessed, I was now reduced to this socially awkward Tolkienian creature.

I followed my yelling with a fast-paced nervous laugh in an attempt to prove I was not from another planet. I don't think this strategy worked particularly well, as the laugh also bellowed out of me with more force than I had intended.

It was kind of like in the movies when a person is mistakenly thrown into an asylum. The more he tries to convince everyone that he's sane, the crazier he seems. It was as if that movie plot were shitting itself out of my mouth in a burst of compulsive chuckles. An "up-chuckle," if you will.

There I was, still squeezing the living Christ out of this Jamaican woman's hand and laughing in tones that sounded like a pregnant horse. I really didn't know where to go from here, so I tried to relax, settle everything down, breathe.

I looked at her quietly, somewhat helplessly. Still squeezing the hand. I tried to form words. For some reason, I could feel tears welling up in my eyes.

"Thank you," I said. "I remember you."

She raised her eyebrows, looking at me as if she wanted to both laugh and run out of the room.

"Look, I know you think I'm a crazy person and you have no idea what I'm talking about right now, but thank you. You were a part of this. And it means a lot to me," I said.

Now the smile behind her mask was unmistakable. A laugh burst out of her, mainly through her nose by the sound of it.

"Okay," she said in her Jamaican accent through the waves of chortling.

She removed her hand from mine, and patted me on the arm. "You sit here as long as you need to."

She left the room and continued laughing down the hall.

None of this struck me at the time as being either positive or negative, comic or solemn, it just *was*.

I sat up slowly and twisted myself around in the chair, preparing to stand up. I realized then, just as my Jamaican friend had alluded, that I would require a few moments of sitting before gaining full use of my legs.

I looked around the room. Everything in it was filled with memory and wonder: the medical instruments, the tiles on the floor, the mindless daytime television droning from the small flat-panel TV suspended from the ceiling. I remembered all of these things. They were all here before I left, and seemed untouched by the vast passing of time. I was delighted to see them again, although I knew it was silly of me.

Just then, the doctor crossed back into the room with his hand extended.

"See!" He exclaimed happily as he shook my hand. "That didn't even feel like forty-five minutes at all, did it?"

My focus sharpened instantly, like a tipsy driver passing a police car. My eyes zeroed in on his, and everything in my being lit up with awareness. In complete sincerity and clarity I squeezed his hand and leaned in close.

"Forty-five minutes? That's...impossible."

"It felt shorter, right?"

"No, no, no," I said, "you don't understand, Doc...I've been gone for almost two hundred years."

There was an odd silence as my dentist just smiled at me, vacantly, his eyebrows raised.

"I just met God."

"We do have a zeal for laughter in most situations, give or take a dentist."

— Joseph Heller

CHAPTER 1:
DOMINO FALLING

I didn't brush my teeth much when I was a kid. I didn't like it. What kid does? Why stand around brushing your teeth when you could be playing video games or destroying your parents' house?

I also didn't shower very much. I'm not proud of it, but there it is. Showering was just as burdensome as tooth brushing. I usually waited for someone to complain about my smell before begrudgingly washing myself. To be fair, I did grow up in the South. As long as you showered before going to church on Sundays, the hygienic sins of the rest of the week might well be forgiven.

I distinctly remember my Aunt Debbie coming over one summer afternoon and embracing my sisters and I, as aunts tend to do, only to push me aside with a contorted face as she told my horrified mother that I stunk. To be fair, Aunt Debbie came from Maryland, which is hardly the South, and either had a more sophisticated sense of smell than the rest of us or a "blue state" sense of hygiene. Or perhaps the rest of us had simply grown accustomed to my boyhood filth; it's neither here nor there. The point is that in a house with two hard-working parents, three children and no housekeepers or nannies, some daily routines simply fell through the cracks.

Of course, tooth brushing – or lack thereof – was a much easier thing to hide than lack of showering. No pesky relatives were getting close enough to my mouth to detect poor dental hygiene. The tactics for avoiding the daily dental scrubbing were relatively simple.

"Did you brush your teeth?" My mother might ask before bedtime.

"Yeah..."

That was pretty much it. I was a highly sophisticated master of deception.

I mean, at that early age, say six or seven years old, what was the advantage of brushing your teeth? Bad breath was the worst of it, I guess. But who cares? I was a geeky little kid with no discernible talents. I knew, even then, that no girl would be kissing me for at least another twenty or thirty years. So bad breath didn't phase me.

Sure, you'd hear adults telling you how "your teeth will rot out if you don't brush them twice a day." But let's put that in perspective, shall we? Adults also said things like, "If you don't eat your carrots, your eyes will go bad." Let me be clear; I like carrots. I eat carrots whenever they are presented to me. I was half-blind by the 5th grade and required giant, googly-eyed bottle glasses to see the Dry Erase board. Do you know why my eyes were so bad? Neither do I, but I'm 85% sure it has nothing to do with carrot consumption. Lies.

"Don't make that face, it will get stuck like that."

I made that face over and over – and it never got stuck like that.

"If you're bad, Santa will bring you coal for Christmas."

Not only was I a perpetually selfish, bratty little shit with no annual coal-like repercussions, but the same people who fed me that lie later confessed that Santa Claus himself wasn't even real.

"What about the tooth fairy?" I remember retaliating when my family finally explained the great Christmas deception to me...at the age of like thirteen.

Nope. There was no tooth fairy, either. Just a bunch of adults making up random stuff, having a blast yanking some kid's chain.

Using outrageous hyperbole in order to teach kids basic life lessons? Fine. Blatantly fabricating various fictional characters in order to pepper a child's early life with magic and wonder and wildly confusing illogic? Sounds like a great plan! That's the world in which this poor, stinky little dork-child grew up. A world of lies.

Well, guess what? The consequence of that low-bar societal standard is that truly clever kids, like myself, learn to adjust. And by "adjust," I mean we learn to not believe a damn thing any adult ever says. My teeth will "rot out" if I don't brush them. Totally. Hey, why don't you get the "tooth fairy" down here to explain that to me in detail, you hacks!

Needless to say, my teeth rotted right out of my disgusting mouth.

My parents were broke as a joke when I was growing up. A kid with cavities represented not only poor dental hygiene, but a serious blow to their checking account – something that I would not fully appreciate for years to come. It was the late 80s and early 90s, so each rotten tooth probably cost about $150-200 to fill.

When I was very young – and I'm talking earliest childhood memories here – I remember my mother sitting me up on the bathroom counter next to the sink and brushing my teeth for me. God, those were the days. A loving and careful woman, my mother's tooth brushing skills kept all three of us cavity-free for years. She took us to the dentist every six months, mainly because her insurance covered two visits per year and my mother does not pass up a deal, especially one that's already been paid for.

The dentist's office was a place where they made us sit with trays in our mouths filled with gooey, bubble-gum flavored fluoride gel for what felt like an hour or two. It seemed like harmless good fun at the time.

It was when we got old enough to brush our own teeth that things took a turn for the worse. At least, it's when I took a turn for the worse. My two other siblings were girls, and at that age I think there is some genetic quirk that makes girls want to be clean. It's weird. They like showering and brushing their hair, etc. The same quirk seems to have the opposite effect on boys. If my parents had considered this back in the late 80s, things might have turned out very differently. Alas, they did not.

I don't remember exactly how old I was. But I do remember sitting in the waiting room at the dentist office after my first "self-brushing" visit. I was in an enormous (regular-sized) wooden chair, my feet nowhere near touching the ground.

The dentist came out with a fistful of x-rays. I can't remember his face, or even if he had a head at all (although, looking back, I suspect he did). All I remember is the classic white "doctor jacket" he was wearing.

"Your son has six cavities," he said matter-of-factly.

My mother's jaw dropped.

I, pleasantly, had no idea what he was talking about.

My mother was usually a happy-go-lucky woman who never showed any cracks in her psychological armor – at least, none that her children could see. But for one brief moment, probably for the first time ever, I saw a flicker of panic streak across her face.

Granted, she might have been disappointed about my dental hygiene, but the panic was purely financial in nature. Six cavities conservatively priced at $150 a pop was a massive amount of money for our family.

"Six?" she asked.

"Six," the doctor said. "I think we should break the fillings up into multiple visits."

My mother nodded, blankly, as she started doing the math in her head, rearranging the family budget for the next six or eight months to cover the unforeseen expense.

There was nothing particularly special about any of these cavities. As far as I know, they were all normal, run-of-the-mill, decaying teeth. Yet, these seemingly routine, insignificant events triggered a life-altering psychological journey.

The day of the first filling, I remember sitting in an enormous (regular-sized) beige dentist chair, complete with that weird craning "dentist light" shining in my face. I can't remember if the dentist tried to explain the procedure beforehand or if he just dove in. As far as I recall, there was no chitchat. The anesthetic needle, the drills, the tiny vacuum for saliva, the metal fillings... on that first day, they were all a complete mystery to me.

(WARNING: If you have a dental phobia, brace yourself. We're about to sail into turbulent waters.)

I remember sitting there, with a pink bib chained around my neck. There was a nurse sitting to my left whose outfit seemed to match the bib. I realize now that "nurse" is the wrong word for a profession known as "dental hygienist," but at the time she looked like a nurse to me, so that's what I'll call her. She wore a face mask and an eye-guard and latex gloves.

The doctor came in, equally geared up, but with the addition of some kind of helmet-contraption on his head. It had a flashlight on it, which made him look as if he were about to go spelunking in my mouth.

The entire spectacle was obviously unsettling, but I kept giving it the benefit of the doubt. Perhaps because for days leading up to this appointment my mother had focused on her disappointment with my tooth brushing skills while down-playing any sense of alarm regarding the cavities themselves. Neither she, nor the dentist or nurses, seemed to have any concerns whatsoever about this procedure. Everything was totally cool. So, naturally, I had no reason to assume there was any sort of danger, despite how foreign everything around me felt in the moment.

I remember seeing the large anesthetic needle in the doctor's hand, coming towards my mouth. Interestingly, this did not terrify me. I wasn't looking forward to the inevitable prick of the needle, but I knew it would be quick enough. And it was. (I found out years later that many people with "dental phobias" are really just afraid of needles. Which is interesting only because it was never the case for me.)

After the anesthetic had been injected, it was protocol in those days to wait about five to ten minutes for the drug to set in, numbing the mouth and teeth. This was a product called "Novocaine," which was the standard numbing agent used in dentistry for most of the twentieth century and into the early 2000s. Within those five or ten minutes, I could feel my cheeks and tongue going numb. It's an odd sensation that you are probably familiar with. It feels like your lips and tongue and skin are puffing up, although they are not. Without the sense of touch, your brain is tricked into registering them almost as foreign objects attached to your face. It's the same feeling as when you wake up in the middle of the night after sleeping on your arm and your hand has fallen asleep; the numbness feels like a dead man's hand lying in bed with you. Novocaine was worse than that, I thought, because it was like the dead man's lips and tongue had been transplanted into your mouth...but I digress.

The point is that I was very well aware that the Novocaine was working, so when the doctor asked, "Can you feel anything?"

"No," I said, honestly.

"Good," he said as he grabbed some metal tool and signaled to the nurse that he was ready to begin.

Now here's where the unforeseen domino falls – the tiny snag that set off the chain of events that constitutes the bulk of this odd memoir. What none of us knew in this moment was that for whatever reason, even though my soft tissue responded to the anesthetic, my teeth themselves were immune to Novocaine. The scientific explanation for this will be explored later. For now, just know that having your teeth drilled without an anesthetic, a whiff of ether or at least a shot or two of whiskey is a torture tactic beyond the scope of even the most nefarious criminal minds.

Within a few moments of the drill connecting with my first tooth, that unmistakable micro-explosion of pain – the kind that only a shrieking tooth can conjure – shot straight into the core of my brain. It was like an icy laser firing directly into the nerve of the tooth. My head twitched to the side, eyes wide open, and I gave a quick series of grunts to the doctor, who stopped the drill.

"Okay. That's alright. The Novocaine hasn't set in yet, we'll give it a few more minutes."

Whew. Okay.

The dentist hit me with another couple shots of Novocaine, just for good measure. Then he and the hygienist dispersed, leaving me alone in the tiny room. I sat for ten or fifteen minutes and waited for my teeth to go numb. A moment that, as it turned out, would never come.

The office was old looking, even for the 80s. The cheap "wood" paneling on the walls gave away that this place was built in the 60s or 70s. And even as a child, I knew that medical offices should appear state-of-the-art and sterile. It was better that way; it offered a sense of confidence in the physicians that faux-wood paneling did not.

I could hear other patients through the corridor having their teeth cleaned. A child started crying loudly somewhere in one of the rooms, perhaps even in the waiting room. I thought how silly it was to cry in a dentist office, a place where doctors and nurses basically just wanted to brush your teeth for you. But I knew that some kids, usually the ones that were younger than me, could be easily frightened by unfamiliar places. Children were funny like that, I thought (not referring to myself, obviously). But I didn't mind this place. I just didn't like the wood paneling.

The waiting felt like quite awhile. My face felt very numb now. I went to scratch my nose and realized that I couldn't feel half of it. "That's a good sign," I thought.

There was a sign on the wall in a little plastic frame that read: "You don't have to floss all your teeth."

I remember thinking, "Oh, that's good, 'cause I don't floss any of them!"

Right below it was another cheaply framed sign that said: "You only have to floss the ones you want to keep."

I felt betrayed. Why were they in two separate frames? What the hell? It was very misleading.

The doctor finally came back into the room followed by the nurse.

"Are you all numb?" he asked with a smile.

I nodded yes and tried to give him an affirmative smile, but half my face was completely numb so I just ended up cracking open one corner of my mouth and grunting a little.

He took a metal pick and started tapping around in my mouth, mainly along the gum line.

"Can you feel this?"

I could not.

"Okay. Let's try this again."

The drill came to life once more. And once more, the pain instantly ripped through me. Searing pain, shooting up my jaw and into my temple.

My head thrashed to the side and my voice wailed reflexively.

"Woah, woah, woah!" The doctor shouted while quickly removing the drill. "If it hurts you can tell me, but you mustn't jerk your head like that!"

The movement seemed involuntary, but I understood what he was getting at. There was a live drill in there, ripping apart my teeth. Thrashing my head around put my whole mouth in jeopardy. I got it. I nodded to the doctor that I understood.

I expected him to give me another couple shots and perhaps let me sit for another few minutes. He didn't.

"Get the bite block, the small one," he said coldly.

The nurse obliged and inserted a faded, dark gray, rubber wedge into my mouth. I was small enough at the time that even the small block was a little too big. As she shoved the wedge back to my molars, it felt like the muscles connecting my jaw to my skull were going to snap, like over-taut guitar strings.

If you're unfamiliar, bite blocks are triangular rubber wedges that force your mouth to stay open. If you fight them, as I did, your muscles tense and your throat closes up. There is also a terribly odd feeling that comes with them... a feeling of being forced. Because your jaw is literally being forced, I suppose.

The doctor instantly began drilling again, and that awful pain shot back up my jawbone. The very roots of my teeth suddenly seemed alive with an icy electric current.

My chest lifted off the chair. My objecting groans turned into a sort of frantic yelping.

The doctor stopped the drill and quickly grabbed the Novocaine needle.

His energy had decidedly shifted now. Over his mask, I could see his cheeks flush with impatience as he began jabbing the needle into my mouth four or five times. I knew he was being haphazard about it this time, not using the careful technique that he had shown before.

Without saying anything to me, he walked to the door and looked down at his watch.

"We'll give him another five minutes, but then we just have to do it."

He left the room.

What did he mean by that? "We just have to do it"?

My heart began racing. I could feel my face, the parts that weren't numb, getting warm and clammy.

I looked over at the nurse. She was already looking at me with sympathy in her eyes, like she knew something that I didn't. I imagine it was something like the way you look at a dog that's about to be put down, although I've never had to do that so I can't say for sure.

We sat in silence. I couldn't think of anything to say that didn't seem childish. And by childish, I mean I couldn't think of anything that didn't admit how scared I was.

I began to tremble.

Trembling with fear was a new sensation for me. It's as if your muscles are telling you that the room is too cold while your skin is telling you the room is too hot. I didn't like trembling.

Despite my fear, I didn't cry. Crying was for children younger than I was. Besides, maybe all those shots he gave me would work this time. I had to hope; it was the only thing that made any sense to do.

The nurse sensed my panic. She tried to soothe me by smiling and rubbing my chest with her hand, the way a mother does to a child in bed with the flu. I imagined that she was probably a good mother. She looked into my eyes and brushed my hair across my forehead.

"It's going to be okay," she said. "You're going to do great." And probably a few other generic affirmations.

I still couldn't think of anything to say in return, so I just looked around the room aimlessly. I quickly tried to calculate what might happen if I leapt out of the chair and ran into the waiting room to explain to my mother that something was very wrong in here. Maybe she'd understand. Maybe she'd think I was being a baby and just throw me back in the chair.

It didn't matter. The five minutes were up.

The doctor returned. This time, he came with another nurse and closed the door behind him.

I knew then that I was in real trouble. I began to sense imminent danger and there was nothing I could do to stop it.

I became hyper-aware of everything around me. My eyes darted around the room, cataloguing every sight, sound and sensation. Every tool on the dentist's tray, the various machines, the cotton swabs, the box of gloves. I looked at the ceiling, I looked at the floor, I looked at the closed door. I looked at the doctor and the two nurses, but none of them would look at me. Not even the nurse who had been comforting me just moments ago.

No one said anything. The nurses knew what to do; they must have been through this before with other kids. The empathetic nurse used one arm to hold my legs while using her other arm to hold my arms and chest down. The new nurse, who was wearing the same pink outfit but with different pajama-looking pants, grabbed my head with both hands and held it rigidly still.

My tiny boyish frame was no match for their adult strength. I was effectively immobilized.

The doctor readied the drill, and went to work.

There were no more subtle grunts or groans that I could use to signal for help. The high-pitched whirring of the drill whistled relentlessly as the agonizing sting cut through me. I screamed. I wailed. My voice opened up with as much sound as I could muster. With hands and wedges and drills in my mouth, I couldn't make words, I could only vocalize. It was a kind of primal, guttural howling. Tears streamed down my face. I cried until my shirt collar was wet, the warm tears pooling at the base of my neck.

I wanted my mother to hear my cries from the waiting room and come running to my rescue. I wanted my father to hear me from his office twenty miles away, drive his car through the terrible wood-paneled walls and grab the dentist by the throat and say, "Get off my son!"

This man was no longer a dentist; he was a villain. Something from a comic book. An evil genius, with pink-coated minions, whose only goal in life was to torture unsuspecting children like me. Surely someone would stop all of this before it went any further. Stories about children in peril never ended like this. But no one came. No friends, no relatives...no heroes. They couldn't. They couldn't hear my screams through the door or over the loud dental machines buzzing and beeping and squealing around the office. I was alone.

I don't know how long this really went on. In realistic terms, I can make an educated guess and say about forty-five minutes or an hour for the two teeth they filled that day. As the doctor had implied, they would drill the cavities out "section by section" according to their groupings in my mouth (two on the upper left, two on the lower right, etc.), each in a separate visit. Therefore, this first round of fillings required three appointments over a period of several weeks.

Each visit was the same. The same steps repeated over and over. Novocaine shots, waiting, more shots, more waiting, holding me down, drilling, screaming, drilling, crying...on and on and on.

One thing did change, though. I learned not to fight it so much. Like the cliché villains always say in bad movies: fighting only makes it worse. I learned to carry toys with me into the room and twist them when the pain started. When that didn't help, I gave up on the toys and just used the arms of the chair or squeezed my own hands.

It's an odd thing, squeezing your own hands in a moment of desperation. It's kind of like in a storybook of Hansel & Gretel or something; the illustrations are always of the two children holding each other's hands as the wicked witch threatens to eat them. It's a natural response to reach out to another person in a bad situation. You want to share the burden and find reassurance. I guess it makes sense then that since I was by myself I would hold my own hands.

This emotional self-reliance became an accidental trademark throughout my childhood and well into my adult life. Funny how these early childhood scenarios can have such resounding effects on all the years that follow.

Maybe you're wondering why my parents kept bringing me back to this man. Well, there were probably a handful of practical reasons, but first you should know that it was not for lack of compassion or for inattentive parenting.

My parents' position was not an easy one. They had to at least consider that my descriptions had been overly dramatized – the normal exaggerations of a child, perhaps. Even so, the reports I gave them of how impossibly painful it all was did not fall on deaf ears. My mother raised concerns about my well-being to the dentist immediately. The trouble was that his views of the events differed from mine.

First, he assured her that he was administering the maximum amount of Novocaine that was legal to inject. (For the record, I have no reason to doubt that this was true. It was a frequent talking point for years to come between myself and other dentists.) Moreover, he told my mother that the pain I was experiencing was a sort of "phantom pain." It was purely psychological. It wasn't real.

Although I had my doubts, who was I to argue with a medical professional? I was probably seven or eight years old. If the doctor said the pain was all in my head, it was probably all in my head, right?

It's also important to note that from my perspective at the time no one else seemed to take my stories about the excruciating dentist pain seriously. My sisters, my friends at school or at church, they all told me, or at least implied, that I was being too sensitive. For example, I remember asking people if it hurt when they went to the dentist and generally, to my surprise and horror, they all said it did!

"Yeah, it hurts a little. It's not comfortable, but you just have to deal with it," was a typical sort of response.

So I assumed everyone was experiencing the same sort of pain that I was experiencing, they just seemed to tolerate it better than I did. Consequently, I stopped telling anyone about what was happening. Even telling my parents just made me feel more childish and weak. If the dentist was right, and the pain was all in my head, it meant that the torture was my own fault. In which case, it seemed better to stop talking about it altogether than to continue to embarrass myself.

Regardless of who was to blame, my parents gave the doctor the benefit of the doubt, and allowed him to finish the six cavities he had been commissioned to fill. I held my toys, and squeezed my hands, and I got through it.

But just in case their son was telling the truth, as soon as the six teeth were repaired my parents never took me or my sisters back to "Dr. Evil," as we now call him.

The psychological scars were carved, but the worst of it was thankfully over.

"The day we fret about the future is the day we leave our childhood behind."

— Patrick Rothfuss

CHAPTER 2:
THE TASMANIAN DEVIL

The next dentist my parents took me to was a funny man with a big mustache. I liked his office because there was no wood paneling. The place was painted white and blue, and the receptionist would always give you a little toy from a cardboard toy chest after each visit. (Literally, it was a cardboard box printed to look like a treasure chest, filled with plastic-wrapped toys like the ones you'd find in a Happy Meal.) There were games to play in the waiting room, like mind puzzles and wooden labyrinths. The kinds of games that are simulated on smartphones and tablets today.

Dr. Mustache was warned in advance that I had experienced "difficulties" with my previous pediatric dentist, so he took extra care to go slowly and stopped drilling whenever I screamed. He was patient with me and told little jokes and funny stories to keep me calm and distracted from the pain. It was still excruciating, but the empathy was nice.

For example, once, he playfully told me to imagine that his dental drill was the "Tasmanian Devil" from *Looney Tunes*. In the cartoon, whenever the Tasmanian Devil got upset, he would spin around so fast that his whole body looked like a little tornado, just like the dental drill looked when it spun around, I guess.

It was a clever ruse. It truly distracted me and made me think about a silly cartoon character as the source of my pain as opposed to the reality of a cold, jagged, metal tool. Of course, the unintended consequence was that for years following this creative imagery I nearly had a panic attack whenever I encountered the Tasmanian Devil on a T-shirt or a TV station.

To be honest, it kind of ruined my taste for the entire *Looney Tunes* franchise. Bugs Bunny and Pepe Le Pew were but casualties in my lifelong War on Dentistry...or dentistry's lifelong war on me.

I'm not sure how many years I saw Dr. Mustache. Several, I suspect. There were a handful of cavities throughout my time with him, despite my renewed respect for the art of tooth brushing. Truthfully though, most of those years are blurry at best. They weren't as traumatic as the first few visits with "Dr. Evil," and therefore their power in my memory is substantially weaker. Nonetheless, I do remember how my time with Dr. Mustache came to an end.

One day the news came that the good dentist had been in a car accident. Don't worry, he survived, but he developed some kind of medical condition that prevented him from practicing dentistry. His hands had a permanent shake or something like that, so I was told.

My mother lamented this news, going on about how such awful things ought not happen to such good people. She was right, of course. They ought not. Yet they so often do. Perhaps this was an early lesson for me about the natural chaos of the Universe, the lack of discernible fairness in the random events of life. As I grew older and bought into the Christian subculture that my family and friends subscribed to, I always knew deep down that this element of universal chaos (and subsequent random suffering) was a serious, unexplainable flaw in the Christian worldview. It was a philosophical quandary that would have greater repercussions later in my life. For now, all I knew was that if any dentist deserved to be in a debilitating car accident it was *Dr. Evil*, not silly old Dr. Mustache.

For a year or two after the accident, there was some hope amongst his staff that he would recover and return to his practice, but he never did. During that purgatory-like interim, his office hired "temporary dentists" to keep his practice going in the hope that Dr. Mustache might return. Regrettably for me, these new doctors turned out not to be doctors at all, but rather rotating student-dentists from the local dental school.

I didn't even know that was legal, but apparently it is. Maybe my parents signed a waiver and got a discount, who knows?

Anyway, remember how Dr. Evil told me not to jerk my head? Well, first of all, I did get a little better at controlling those reflexes over the years. But sometimes, instinct takes over and there's nothing that can be done. Now, unlike Dr. Evil, who at least had a quick hand and could shut down the dental equipment at the first sign of trouble (if he wanted to), the dental students were less prepared for mishaps or, well, sudden movements.

There I was, with Dr. Dental Student, little twelve-year-old me, desperately trying not to scream bloody murder in my very large (regular-sized) dental chair while having another cavity filled. The drill was painfully cutting into my tooth when it hit an especially vulnerable nerve and my head jerked to the side, as it was wont to do. Unfortunately, Dr. Dental Student left the drill running as he nervously tried to evacuate my mouth. The end result was that he drilled a hole straight through my bottom lip.

Luckily, although my teeth were in excruciating pain, my lips and face were completely numb. I would never have thought anything was wrong if the drill hadn't made a funny flesh-grinding sound and Dr. Dental Student's eyes hadn't gotten so wide. Of course, the blood spilling all over my baby blue plastic bib was also a sure sign of trouble.

For the record, this was the last time I used the imagery of the Tasmanian Devil during my adventures in dentistry. Once a *Loony Tunes* character draws blood, you've pretty much graduated to an age of more practical metaphors and distractions.

This was also understandably the last time my parents took me to Dr. Dental Student, and the last time I saw Dr. Mustache's office.

The next stop on my journey was a dental office in the next town over, nearly a forty-five minute drive from our house. The doctor was a short, pleasant man from Idaho. Let's call him Dr. Idaho.

I remember going through all of the same routines with him as I had with the previous dentists – Novocaine shots, waiting, drilling, pain, more shots, more waiting, more drilling, more pain, etc. The big difference here was that Dr. Idaho was not a pediatric dentist, so his mind-set was very different. He explained things to me openly and thoroughly, almost as if talking to a real adult (no cartoon references, for example). This full-disclosure approach made me feel strangely better, despite my continuing fear of the drill.

I was getting older, becoming a teenager, and Dr. Idaho and his staff helped foster a sense of self-awareness and maturity in me that I had not previously known. I realized that I could be honest with them about the pain I was experiencing without feeling somehow "overly sensitive" or, well, childish.

Looking back, I'm well aware that this was a healthy step forward. It was the beginning of a slowly growing self-realization…as well as an emotional tinderbox just waiting to be ignited.

After a few years of treatment, including several more painful fillings, I remember telling Dr. Idaho that my pediatric dentist had suggested that my pain was purely imaginary. Surprisingly, he seemed to think that this was unlikely. I, of course, was easily persuaded to agree with him. He was the first dentist to suggest that my teeth may not be receptive to Novocaine (or its sister drug, a similar product called "Lidocaine"). I wasn't aware that such a condition existed, but essentially the idea is that the nerves in my teeth were positioned in slightly abnormal ways that restricted or prevented the effective use of those particular anesthetic agents.

I also probably just had sensitive teeth. The very idea of chewing an ice cube, for example, still raises the hair on the back of my neck. When I was a child, I was thoroughly amazed at such feats of bravery and dental fortitude. This was the stuff of legend, like swallowing swords and spitting fire. Little did I know that some people just had less sensitive teeth than I did. This made me lose respect for ice chewers everywhere, but it also relieved my non-ice-chewing inferiority complex.

All of this new information about science and abnormal nerve endings (and ice chewing) were a revelation for me. It was the opening of a whole new chapter in my dental journey. I was becoming truly aware of the intense level of pain I was experiencing with each drilling, because now I had knowledge on my side, validating those torturous experiences. When you're a teenager, knowledge always makes you feel older and wiser, so in a strange way, I was beginning to feel like more of an adult.

What I didn't know was that I had an adult-sized fear developing inside my brain. A fear that was becoming larger than just the pain itself.

Granted, everyone fears pain. We are evolutionarily hardwired for this response, presumably for self-preservation. It is a rational basic instinct. But, without being self-aware enough to know it, my fear had seeped into less rational places. In fact, it had seeped into nearly everything. Every sight, every sound, every smell I associated with the dentist's office sent a wave of panic through me. Like an army of fire ants trapped inside my brain, desperately trying to gnaw their way out. This was a crippling mental state. But worse than that, worse than any of the needles or drilling, was the paralyzing fear of hearing these four catalytic words: "You have a cavity."

My fear of hearing those words had grown so large that, for weeks leading up to even a simple cleaning, I would lose my appetite, I couldn't sleep and I'd have difficulty concentrating at school.

I knew it was becoming a real problem, but never really discussed it with anyone. Discussing one's problems with others was inadvertently discouraged where I grew up. I say inadvertently because I believe that this feeling of solitude and isolation is one of the unintended consequences of my belief in Christianity at the time.

Allow me to explain. A belief that God alone can truly solve your problems can lead to a kind of emotional isolation for the believer. It's the belief that humans are, by nature, powerless, weak and soiled with sin, and subsequently that God *alone*, in all His wisdom and mercy, has the power to heal you through prayer and humility. Any other means of so-called "self help" falls short of the glory of God and only leads the believer further away from divine truth…further away from God. And anything that leads a Christian away from God is inherently a path towards wickedness.

With this foolproof theory in tow, why bother telling anyone else about my embarrassing fear of dentistry? All I needed to do was turn to God. So, that's all I did.

I attended a typical Southern Baptist Church twice a week and was very active in the youth group and praise choir. I prayed daily with honest thanksgiving and humble reflection. In times of trouble, like going to the dentist, I prayed even harder than usual.

"Protect my teeth, O Lord, for they have sinned. Yea, though I walk through the valley of oral decay, I will fear no dentist. Thy kingdom come, thy enamel be redone. With fluoride and sugar-free gum, as it is in Heaven. In the name of the Father, the Son, Crest, Colgate and Oral-B. Amen."

That's an example of what I might have prayed prior to entering the dentist's office.

Of course, every time I *left* the dentist's office, my prayer was more along the lines of: "God, O God, why have you forsaken me?"

Perhaps dentistry was in one of God's blind spots. Or worse, perhaps God heard my cries, but allowed me to suffer in order to punish me for some spiritual misdemeanor or other. In my superstitious mind at the time, it was a totally valid possibility.

Whether it was a product of poor childhood hygiene or bad genetics, I had almost as many fillings in my mouth as I had teeth by the end of it. I was brushing twice a day and flossing and rinsing with fluoride and avoiding hard candy and soda, but the cavities just kept coming, year after year.

I truly began to believe that it had nothing to do with bacteria or acidic food/drink or even daily hygiene; the science behind my cavities and my anti-cavity behavior just wasn't lining up. So I began to suspect that something supernatural was afoot. It was a punishment from God. It was the only thing that made any sense. These cavities could have been his way of smiting me for being too selfish or laughing at too many inappropriate jokes at school. Who knew? Either way, I felt awfully smited. Thoroughly smote, in fact.

Although there were other kids at school who I *knew* were way worse than me, they had fewer cavities than I did – and they probably didn't even floss! They could crush ice with their teeth and everything. It was incredibly unfair. It was so confusing and spiritually exhausting.

Again, I think the philosophical foundation of understanding chaos in an unjust Universe was being laid beneath my unsuspecting feet.

And then, one day, without warning, it happened: the spark in the tinderbox.

I was around sixteen-years-old. I had just finished a routine dental exam with Dr. Idaho. After reviewing some x-rays and jabbing a terrifying metal hook around in my mouth, he said the dreaded words.

"You. Have. A. Cavity."

It felt like time suspended and the lights dimmed and maybe some footlights appeared and cast eerie shadows across Dr. Idaho's round face. My whole body tensed up. The panic of another procedure with the craning light and the saliva vacuum and the bite block and all those sounds and the taste of the oral anesthetic and the latex gloves, and the needle, and the excruciating drill carving into my teeth – all of it flooded into my mind. Terror set in, and something deep inside of me just...snapped.

"No," I said quickly.

There was a pause.

"No?" he asked.

"I'm not going to let you fill the cavity."

The dentist just stared at me blankly.

"I would rather let the tooth rot and fall out on its own than have the drill again. I can't do it, Doc. I'm sorry, I just can't."

I tried to stop it from happening, but my eyes filled with water. Tears from an array of emotions that were suddenly surging through me: the fear of having to potentially endure one more absurdly painful dental procedure, the embarrassment of having to admit out loud that my fears had grown so overwhelming, the pride of finally standing up for myself and stopping the seemingly endless cycle of torment that had replayed itself over and over since I was a child.

If God couldn't put an end to all this, I would.

"No."

The doctor took this in.

Without saying a word, he reached for a prescription pad and began scribbling.

"Josh, I'm going to give you some pills that will help with the anxiety you're experiencing. I want you to take one tonight when you go to bed and take the other in the morning about an hour before coming back here."

"Okay," I said, "but what do the pills do? Will it just help with anxiety, or will it stop the actual pain?"

He thought about it for a moment, which made me suspicious. Then he said, "Yes, it will help with the pain, too. I promise you, you won't feel a thing."

I didn't know if I could really trust him, but for the first time ever in my dental journey, there was hope!

"It's always darkest just before
they turn on the lights."

— P.G. Wodehouse

CHAPTER 3:
DAWNING OF THE AGE OF AQUARIUS

I got the prescription filled immediately and ran home as fast as I could. (Not literally. I had a car. We weren't *that* Southern.)

I stared at the pill bottle. It was tiny. A small orange canister with only two pills in it, but it felt like the pharmacist had filled that beautiful little vial with hope itself, in tablet form.

Printed on the label were the instructions that Dr. Idaho had given me earlier. "Take one before bed and one in the morning prior to your dental procedure." Next to this label was a bright red sticker with a picture of a martini glass with an "X" over it. The sticker read, "Taking this medication with alcohol may increase the effects of the medication."

"No problem there," I reckoned. "I never drink alcohol anywa– WAIT."

I reread the sticker: "...may increase the effects of the medication"?

"This is no warning," I thought. "This is a recommendation."

It was midnight. My parents had gone to bed over half an hour ago. I quickly and quietly poured a glass of white wine – the low-quality grocery store stuff that my mother had in the fridge. I prepared to wash down the first pill before anyone caught me.

To be very clear, drinking alcohol, even wine, was strictly forbidden in our house on account of the rules of the Southern Baptist Church. My mother enjoyed a wine cooler or an occasional glass from time to time, but even this small consumption perturbed my father to no end. He was much more religious than my mother. In fact, Dad was a Sunday School teacher and a choir member (baritone-tenor) and took everything to do with the Southern Baptist Church *very* seriously. (To be fair, so did I at the time.)

Southern Baptists, for those of you who may not know, are forbidden to drink any alcohol for any reason. The theory is, as my father explained on more than one occasion, that even if you don't have a problem with alcohol, it might be a "spiritual stumbling block" for others. All church members, therefore, are expected to observe total abstinence.

Of course, the logic of this is painfully obtuse. First of all, Jesus himself drank wine, according to – oh, I dunno – *the Bible*. So they're essentially suggesting that the Southern Baptist organization has a better standard of morality than Jesus Christ himself. Moreover, the logic of removing every possible stumbling block from every possible path is a maddening downward spiral that is, obviously, unsustainable. People are addicted to cigarettes, computers, TVs, tanning beds and God knows what else. Should everyone always avoid all of those things, too? Where does the illogic end? I digress. The point is that dad was highly uncomfortable with having alcohol in the house. The idea that I was abusing prescription drugs with said alcohol was nothing short of pure wickedness. This was highly dangerous territory, and I had to be cautious and quick.

Then, a new thought occurred to me. I looked at the pharmacy label again.

"Take one before bed and one in the morning."

"Why?" I thought. "I don't need help with pain and anxiety while I'm sleeping. I need it tomorrow."

Flashes of brilliance streaked across my mind. The perfect plan was hatched!

I poured the wine back into the bottle and went straight to bed – without taking anything.

The next morning, a sunny, summer Friday, as my mother prepared to drive me to the dentist's office, I stealthily poured a glass of wine and chugged it with *both* of the pills.

I checked the time. Just past eight a.m. The appointment was for nine o'clock. It takes forty minutes to get there. Everything was right on schedule.

I was still shaky and nervous as we began our journey. I had never taken any sort of anxiety medication before, so I had no idea how it worked or what to expect. In fact, I had never taken much medication of any kind.

All I knew was that right now, in this car, on my way to a dental filling with my new anxiety medication, I was still feeling quite anxious.

But whatever. "Life is short, right?" I thought to myself. "Don't worry about it. Everything will sort itself out. Just take it easy and breathe, Josh. Just watch the houses and trees go by. Try to enjoy this calm before the dental storm. Gosh, that morning sun is bright. Close those eyes, my friend, and let your mind wander. Don't care where it goes, as long as it's a happy place. Come to think of it, I don't care about much of anything right now... and this car feels pretty happy...oooh...uh-oh."

Darkness descended.

I woke up in my bed. At first I thought it was mid-afternoon and that I must have returned from the dentist and slept for an hour or two. But as I looked out my bedroom window, the sun was decidedly in its mid-morning position.

"That can't be right," I thought. "Did I even go to the dentist?"

It began to feel a little like *Groundhog Day*.

I ran my tongue over my teeth. Sure enough, there was a rough patch of newly paved dental composite.

I checked my phone. It was Saturday morning.

"What happened to the last twenty-four hours??"

On my nightstand where my phone had been, I noticed a yellow sticky-note with the words "Call Lauren" written in my own handwriting.

Stranger still, I'd gotten a new cell phone several months earlier and lost all of my contacts (the "cloud" didn't exist in those days). I hadn't spoken to my friend Lauren in months and didn't have her phone number.

Half asleep, I flipped open my phone (cell phones used to flip open). Lo and behold, under the "recent calls" tab was Lauren's name.

Bewildered, I redialed the number.

"Hello?" She answered with odd hesitation.

"Lauren?"

She burst into laughter. "Ohmigod, you don't remember talking to me at all yesterday, do you?"

Uh-oh. This could be bad.

Full disclosure, I had a solid crush on Lauren. Of course, I was sixteen, so I had a solid crush on everything that moved. And Lauren, like most girls I had ever known, had made it very clear that we were strictly platonic. If I was having conversations with her in some kind of drug-induced anti-anxiety state, who knows what I might have told her?! Thankfully, she seemed to be in non-awkward spirits, so maybe I was safe from total hormonal-teenager-on-drugs embarrassment.

"We talked yesterday?" I choked lamely on a half-laugh.

"Yes! I got your number from Caitlin, but you were totally out of it! You weren't making any sense. I asked what was wrong and you told me this whole thing about your dentist giving you drugs and how you couldn't tell what day it was. Then you just got...weird."

Uh-oh.

"What do you mean, 'got weird'?" I asked.

"I don't know. You just stopped making sense."

Okay. As long as "got weird" wasn't code for "told me you wanted to lose your virginity," I was fine with it.

"You were totally gone," she continued, "so I made you put my number into your phone and write yourself a note to call me when the drugs wore off."

We caught up for a bit and laughed about all the funny non-sequiturs from the day before. I was just as amused as she was at the goofy antics, but moreover, I was overjoyed that the pills had worked! I didn't remember *anything* from the cavity filling! Granted, erasing a solid twenty-four hours of my memory was overkill, but this was by far the best dentist visit I had ever had! It was completely pain-free!

This system was perfect! As long as I had a chaperone and knew I wouldn't drive my car off a cliff or something, what's the worst that could happen?

I got off the phone and jumped out of bed, still a bit groggy but ecstatic at this new prospect of a torture-free life.

I stepped into the bathroom, as one often does in the morning, and without warning, my day took a decidedly bizarre turn for the worse.

(WARNING: Viewer discretion is advised.)

Standing over the familiar toilet was an incredibly unfamiliar sight. All of my pubic hair was gone.

Gone.

All of it.

It was not a particularly close shave, but more of a reckless hack job. Like when you cheap out on the landscaping service and just pay the kid down the street twenty bucks to mow your lawn. I'm probably lucky that my hair was the only thing missing.

Lesson one: Don't cheap out on landscaping services.

Lesson two: My drugged-out remedy for escaping dentistry was apparently not without its consequences.

I was stunned. This was, after all, in an era when personal

grooming of this kind was neither common nor openly discussed. Where the idea even came from to perform such an act, even on a subconscious level, still escapes me to this day.

My eyes quickly darted around the room looking for clues as to what had happened here – perhaps any evidence of a struggle or foul play. All I found was an enormous electric razor (I think it was the one we used to shave the dog during the summer) and a mound of pubic hair in the wastebasket. It was not discreetly disposed of either, the way a savvy manscape artist might manage after a grooming session. No, this was loud and proud. Someone had brazenly shaved their pubis and displayed the fruits of their labor grossly on top of the nearly full wastebasket. And that someone was me. I was both disgusted and impressed.

What on earth had compelled me to *do* this? Why couldn't I remember anything? What else did I do while on these pills?

On the other hand, who cared?? I got a cavity filled for the first time in my life with absolutely no pain! Who needs pubic hair??

I found my mother in the kitchen and asked her to fill me in on any details she could remember. After laughing a bit at my sluggish, dopey antics, she told me about the procedure itself.

"You basically slept through it," she said, "which you're not supposed to do. You're supposed to be relaxed, not asleep! The doctor thinks your body is too sensitive to the drug he gave you."

Too sensitive? Ha. Too reckless with prescription drug abuse, perhaps, but that would remain my little secret for the time being.

In case you're curious, while writing this book I did some online research to find out exactly what *had* happened that day (and by "online research," I mean I did *a* Google search). The drug he gave me was most likely something in the benzodiazepine family (a group commonly known as "benzos"). This family includes drugs like Valium, Xanax and Ativan. In normal doses, these drugs have a calming effect. This is the "anti-anxiety" outcome that Dr. Idaho was aiming for. In larger doses, their effects are far more acute, inducing something that the medical field calls a "sedative-hypnotic effect."[3] That is, they make your brain half-asleep (sedative) and half-awake, or in a state of minimal consciousness (hypnosis), similar to the effects of heavy alcohol or opium consumption. Taking alcohol with the benzodiazepine, as I did, compounds the effect.

"So," my mother continued, "he's going to reduce the dosage if you ever have to use them again."

In my mind, I let out a Darth-Vader-style "Nooooooo!" And yet, despite my disapproval of reducing future dosages, a part of me understood that it was probably for the best. After all, this whole experience had felt like a pretty close shave. (Again, I feel disgusted and impressed with myself, for writing that joke. I apologize. And you're welcome.)

A year or two later, Dr. Idaho fulfilled his threat. He cut my dosage in half. I still took both pills the morning of the procedure with a glass of wine. The result of the decreased dosage was that instead of blacking out for twenty-four hours, I only blacked out for about twelve.

I'm also happy to report that after the first incident, there was no more hair loss, in case you were wondering.

Dr. Idaho wanted to cut my dose again after my second filling because I slept through most of the procedure again. So I confessed to him privately that the pills themselves weren't the problem, but that I was taking them incorrectly and with alcohol to purposefully intensify their effect. He was surprisingly understanding of what I had done, but told me that if I came back again unable to stay awake he would be forced to reduce the dosage for my own good.

The next time I saw him, I discontinued the alcohol, but still took both pills at once. I didn't want to risk going back to the days of anguish and torture that I dreaded from my childhood.

Sans alcohol, the two pills were still powerful enough to put me to sleep for the better part of eight hours or so, but I found that I could hang onto consciousness just enough to get through the fillings without the dentist's disapproval. And so, this was the pattern of my dental experiences for almost a decade thereafter, essentially throughout all of high school and college.

It wasn't a perfect solution, I'll admit, but it worked. And the pubic hair story was a huge hit at more than one college party.

Even though my school was 700 miles away from my hometown, I was too scared of seeing any other dentists for fear that they wouldn't give me the "forgetting drugs," so I waited to see my dentist back home on holidays or summer vacations.

It wasn't until I finished college and moved to a new city that I was forced to leave Dr. Idaho behind and find a new dentist all on my own.

I was terrified.

"Answer me quickly, O Lord, my spirit fails. Hide not your face from me, lest I be like those who go down to the pit."

—Psalm 143:7

CHAPTER 4:
THE LIFE AND DEATH OF A GOD

I don't know exactly how or when it happened. One day, I just turned around and God was gone. My faith was gone. The sensation that some magical being was walking through life with me, sympathizing with my existential wailings and thanksgivings, guiding me towards some destiny that was designed especially for me…it was all gone. In its place, there was only the cold reality that I was alone in a chaotic universe, spinning haplessly into oblivion.

There was no singular traumatic event that caused this, but perhaps a series of them over the course of my young adult life in combination with a growing sense of theological illogic that no amount of "Christian apologetics" could sate.

When I was very young, I naturally believed whatever my parents chose for me to believe. Adam & Eve lived in a garden where a snake told them to do bad things because it was possessed by a demon. One day it rained so hard the entire planet flooded because God was mad at people and wanted to kill them all, except the one family He told to build a boat. Jesus was born half-man/half-God and was murdered because he wanted people to celebrate Christmas and Easter.

It all made sense to me as child, because the adults around me said it made sense.

That is, until I discovered that Santa Claus, the Easter Bunny and the Tooth Fairy didn't exist. Those characters were all equally magical to me as God or Jesus were. In fact, I had seen more hard evidence of Santa than of "God." Jesus never brought me presents or replaced my teeth with dollar bills in the middle of the night. Naturally, when those lying adults explained that none of the holiday characters were real, I assumed that God and Jesus belonged to that same fictitious camp.

In the years that followed, it boggled my mind that my parents and others continued to talk about Jesus as if he were a historical figure. Once I understood the concept of Hell, the idea of God became even more unbelievable. God was apparently just like Santa, except that instead of deciding whether or not to bring you presents, He was making a "naughty or nice" list in order to determine whether or not to set you on fire for eternity.

"Why on earth would anyone want to believe this stuff?!" I thought.

Therefore, I shrugged off Christianity for a few years, roughly between the ages of 8 and 14. As a consequence, I noticed that my very pro-Christian father had grown increasingly disapproving and distant from me and my two sisters, who seemed equally unimpressed with Christianity. He began spending most of his leisure time at Church, doing God only knows what (literally). His subtle isolation away from the family angered me, even at that young age, and I began to instinctually link the lack of my father's attention with the Church, which made me angry at the Church itself, and even at the very idea of God.

Then, one summer, I was reluctantly sent to a Bible Camp where an adolescent Christian girl asked me, somewhat innocently, "If you don't believe in God, what do you think will happen to you when you die?" I had no answer, which only gave the young evangelizer more ammunition. "If you don't know what will happen when you die, isn't it better to believe in God, in case it turns out that the Bible is right? That way you'll be sure not to go to Hell!"

Boom. I was *sold*!

Christianity was back on the menu, even if only as a sort of afterlife insurance policy. Looking back, I'm ashamed to admit that such simplistic fear-baiting worked on me, but in my defense, I was in middle school.

Remarkably, my relationship with my self-estranged father immediately reversed course. Suddenly I understood him, and he understood me! With great pride, I became the favorite son, and not just because I was the only son.

We spent hours in Bible study, with Dad giving me crash courses in theology and apologetics. We sang in church together, side by side as father and son. We went to rallies in Washington, D.C., together, and prayed on the steps of the U.S. Capitol for Congress to heed God's call.

Was my father's renewed investment in me simply because I had conformed to his religious interests, or because *God* was blessing me with closeness to my father? Obviously, I suspected the latter.

I became heavily involved in the Church. In addition to singing, I was a youth group leader and a Christian ambassador to many multicultural camps and programs – not to better understand other cultures, mind you, but to attempt to spread Christianity to the uninitiated. One summer, I spent a week in Chicago evangelizing in the city's ghettos, where you couldn't wear certain colors without accidentally aligning yourself with one gang or another. When a man frantically tried to stop me from entering one particularly dangerous neighborhood for fear that I might be shot merely for having white skin, I replied calmly, "When God is on our side, who can stand against us?"[4] This is how deeply entrenched my faith had become.

From here, my downward spiritual journey is pretty mundane and commonplace. I simply left home, and saw more of the world.

I spent a summer abroad studying music. I attended an out-of-state residential high school program for the arts. I went to college in Boston.

I met hundreds of new people from all walks of life, many of whom had dramatically different social and spiritual backgrounds. Some of these people appeared equally passionate and fulfilled by their chosen faiths as I had been in mine. I could detect something in them – a kind of spiritual peace and fortitude that I had previously only attributed to my devout Christian brethren. The realization of this put cracks in the foundation of my spiritual beliefs, which inherently presumed divine superiority above all other religions.

I could not, in good conscience, admit that my religion instructed me to believe that all of these people were worshipping "false gods" and thusly condemned to Hell. This was a source of major spiritual conflict for me that went unresolved for many years.

What's more, I met homosexual couples who had been committed to one another for decades, raising children together in loving homes. This was no illusion of love; this was unmistakably real, a palpable connection between people, no different than the most supportive heterosexual couples and their families. In short, it wasn't the foul, sex-crazed, heathen attack on God and country that many of my fellow Christians were clamoring about. But I was supposed to believe these people were going to Hell? It didn't make sense. It didn't feel right. It just resulted in more spiritual conflict.

Then I began feeling suffocated by practical issues with the faith. For example: how do we know for sure who really wrote the original books of the Bible? If Jesus's message was so important to him, why didn't he write it down himself? Why did God create a universe in which people go to Hell if they don't choose to worship him? Should we ignore global warming in case it's just part of God's plan to destroy the earth like in the Book of Revelation? Augh!!

As you can see, this is a rabbit hole.

Nevertheless, I continued to identify as a Christian, though I often found myself trying to distance myself from it. I didn't like using the word "Christian," because I began to sense its negative connotations. Negative because many believers made their faith a platform for hatred against any point of view that differed from their own. This seemed to apply to virtually any subject – not only religion and morality, but also science, government, education and so on. I became embarrassed, not of Christ, but of Christians.

After college, professional life took off like a rollercoaster, with extreme highs and even more extreme lows. In the midst of trying to emotionally and spiritually navigate my own life events, I became increasingly burdened by the trials of others, and how irrefutably random it all seemed. Christians were just as likely to lose their jobs or be diagnosed with cancer as non-Christians. They were just as likely to be killed in car accidents. People who prayed to Jesus to save their ailing loved ones were just as likely to watch their loved ones die as Muslims, Jews, Hindus or Atheists.

On a personal level, I simply couldn't ignore that my odds of good or bad fortune had no correlation with my devotion to God. I could pray all night and selflessly submit myself to the callings of the Lord, but nothing changed my odds of receiving a statistically balanced share of good, bad and ugly.

Not that I was testing God in any way, I was only making observations in retrospect and connecting the dots. I mean, shouldn't your worship of an all-powerful God have some kind of benefit beyond merely helping you cope with the good and bad fortunes that life throws at you? Shouldn't your God have some physical effect on your life, presumably a positive one? Even if you remove religion from the equation altogether and just look at it from a colloquially "karmic" standpoint, why do good people have bad fortune while bad people have good fortune, not only in money, but in love and health and happiness? It just doesn't make much sense in the narrative of a passionate, interactive God who rewards righteousness over wickedness.

And I guess that's when I noticed it. After one particularly brutal personal setback, I turned to scream at the heavens, and it hit me – there was nothing there. I was screaming at a God that either didn't care, wasn't listening or wasn't there. Either way, I had spent enough years chasing after Him and coming up short.

I was tired of feeling not good enough to deserve God's love or attention. His lack of affection towards me should have come as no surprise. After all, He peppered His book with verses about how undeserving we all are of Him.

It was not lost on me that during this time, as my connection with the divine faded away, my connection with my father followed suit. What had once been a profound bond over our similar beliefs had descended into a profound separation over our differences. We could scarcely hold a private conversation that didn't quickly escalate into an argument. Whenever the two of us sat down together, the rest of the family would leave the room, presumably to get out of the blast radius. We spent hours debating each other – me attacking his primitive superstitions and fundamentalist hypocrisy, him attacking my self-righteous moral relativism and baseless agnosticism.

This freshly repeated cycle of separation from my father only fueled my bitterness towards God and the Church. Once again, it felt as though my father had stepped behind the comfortable curtain of Christianity and pulled it shut behind him.

It wasn't that Dad was intentionally turning his back on me, though it almost would have been easier if he had. I could have attacked him for that kind of deliberate betrayal. Rather, it was an instinctual, habitual withdrawal, completely devoid of malice, which somehow made it all the more painful.

Whatever resentment I had towards my father over such things, or towards my career, or the unfairness of the world at large, it all paled in comparison to my resentment towards God. I was angry that He'd hidden my father away from the family. I was angry that He seemed so aloof and silent in the times that I needed Him most. I was angry that He seemed to relish how confusing and difficult it was for humans to believe in Him.

Moreover, if there was a God out there, I wanted Him to know that I was completely reversing the roles on Him. I wanted Him to know how disappointed *I* was in *Him*. How undeserving He was of my devotion.

In a way, it was very freeing. It was like breaking up with an abusive partner. Imagine a spouse who claimed to love you unconditionally, yet berated you and constantly told you how awful and undeserving you were, insisted that he was listening to your voicemails even though he never actually responded to them, and then threated you with endless torture if you challenged him or asked to leave. It felt like that was the relationship I was finally ending.

It felt fantastic.

It felt terrifying, because I knew there'd never be another relationship like it. My days with religion had ended.

This was the bitter, desolate spiritual place I found myself in when I met Him – God, the almighty Creator of the Universe.

Funnily enough, my dentist introduced us.

"YOU HAVE TO TAKE SERIOUSLY THE NOTION THAT UNDERSTANDING THE UNIVERSE IS YOUR RESPONSIBILITY, BECAUSE THE ONLY UNDERSTANDING OF THE UNIVERSE THAT WILL BE USEFUL TO YOU IS YOUR OWN UNDERSTANDING."

— TERENCE MCKENNA

CHAPTER 5:
LIFT OFF

I moved to New York City in late 2004. The city can be a scary, overwhelming place for a recent college graduate. Some wiser man than I once said that New York has "the best and the worst of everything." After living there for only a couple years, I was convinced that this was true. From Saks Fifth Avenue to the semi-legal Chinatown boutiques, from Delmonico's downtown to the semi-legal "street meat" in Times Square – the best and the worst of everything, together in perfect harmony.

Naturally, I assumed that if the best, most sympathetic, most skilled dentist in the world lived anywhere, he lived in New York. Likewise, if the worst, most brutal, unskilled, barbaric dentist in the world lived anywhere, he was also probably a subway ride away. Because of this, I was fully prepared to forgo any kind of dental maintenance until I was confident that I had found the former.

By kindness of fate, after many months of half-hearted but mandatory searching, I found him. Let's call him Dr. Fantastic.

When I stepped into Dr. Fantastic's office for the first time, I instantly knew that I had found the right place. The walls were covered with pictures of him and various celebrities. There were major magazine articles featuring his practice framed all around the waiting room. His website boasted about how he frequently spoke at national dental conferences, and highlighted his contributions to reality "makeover" programs on network television. This guy was the real deal.

That, and they told me over the phone that they'd give me anti-anxiety drugs to get me through my dental phobia. Sold!

For the record, I don't call him Dr. Fantastic just because he promised an anxiety-free experience. He actually looked kind of like a superhero. Pristinely coiffed brown hair, pleasantly tanned skin, a peerless gym body and a permanent politician's smile with perfect, pearly white teeth (naturally).

Even the dental hygienist I was paired with was fantastic! She was a remarkably compassionate and understanding woman who could not have been gentler while I was in the exam chair. She understood that I was tense and at my most vulnerable, and treated me as if I were her own nervous child. Which meant a lot to me, given that when I was actually a child, I didn't get that kind of compassion from folks in her line of work.

It had been several years since my last dental visit. I was not entirely surprised that a cavity had developed by the time I met Dr. Fantastic. Nevertheless, I froze upon hearing those diabolical words fall from his oddly heroic lips.

"You have a cavity."

My heart skipped a beat. Fate seemed to be confirming my recently adopted belief that God did not, in fact, exist.

He pointed to an x-ray image on a fancy computer screen, showing me a slightly discolored area on a large tooth in the back of my mouth. My hands became clammy and my flesh paled. I was faced with the inevitable task of discussing the gory details of the forthcoming procedure, namely whether or not he could give me the roofie-style drugs that I had grown accustomed to.

I explained to him that in the past, I usually didn't remember anything about the procedures or the hours that followed them. He looked at me curiously. Obviously, I didn't tell him anything about my doubling-down on the pills or the alcohol. I didn't want to start our relationship off with him knowing how much of a problem child I was, though he would find out soon enough.

"I don't know what you would have taken that would have done that. But no, nothing we use has that extreme of an effect."

Terror instantly began to set in as I realized I may have walked into a trap.

"We'll give you a Xanax half an hour before your appointment. Do you really think you'll need more than that for just a filling?"

"IT'S A TRAP!!" I screamed inside my mind. "This is a classic bait and switch!! They said they'd dope me up, but all they meant was one fucking Xanax?! I can't even double-dose it with alcohol if they give it to me in the office!! What do I do!?"

Sirens blared and everything in my geek-brain began flashing red as the Starship Captain of my mind ordered me to raise shields and warp-speed my ass out of this liar's office.

But instead, I made one last attempt to reason with this man and his now notably concerned dental hygienist.

"I don't think you understand. I don't handle this stuff well. I don't know if I can do it."

Again, he looked at me curiously.

"Did you have any bad experiences with dentists when you were a kid?" he asked.

"How did he know??" I thought, mystified, still not really understanding that phobias were diagnosable mental conditions that doctors actually knew about.

For the record, this was the first time anyone had asked me about my childhood dentist visits. In fact, I had not actually thought about those memories in years, mainly because I didn't want to face them. I didn't really even connect those experiences with the fears I had as an adult. I just assumed that my teeth were sensitive and Novocaine didn't work on me. In other words, I thought it was a rational fear of the potential pain. I had not yet come to understand the true nature of a *phobia*, which was an *irrational* fear. In my case, as with many cases, this phobia was based on sense-memory associations from my childhood that lurked deep in my subconscious. Somewhere inside my mind was a six-year-old boy, terrified of being tortured again.

A therapist many years later was the first to actually identify these symptoms of post-traumatic stress that I had been unknowingly carrying around for decades. I had only ever associated that phrase with soldiers returning from war, but its definition is actually much broader.

Some psychologists don't even believe that odontophobia (or dentophobia, or "dental anxiety") actually exists. Instead, they believe there is a more specific condition called "Post-traumatic Dental-care Anxiety" (PTDA), which is akin to the broader term "Post-Traumatic Stress Disorder" (PTSD).[5]

In my mid-twenties, however, I knew nothing of these psychoanalytic theories. All I knew was the panic and the embarrassment that I was feeling in the moment.

"Yes," I said, slowly coming out of the fog in my mind. "I had some pretty awful shit go down when I was a kid. Novocaine doesn't work on me. It never has. But they held me down and drilled on me anyway."

Everything in my body clenched just saying these words out loud for the first time in so long.

"I understand," Dr. Fantastic said calmly. "Almost everyone I see who has a dental phobia had bad experiences as a child. It is very common. When was the last time you had a filling?"

"I don't know. It's been at least a few years. Why?"

"Because we only use the latest drugs and technology. I haven't used Novocaine since the early 2000s. The last time you had a cavity filled, did it take ten minutes or so for the numbness to set in?"

"Well, the numbing never totally sets in for me," I said, "but yes, I always had to wait awhile."

"Okay. That was Novocaine. We don't use that. We use a product called Septocaine. It's much more effective and works instantly. Within a few seconds, you won't feel anything."

I took a moment to process this information. Faster doesn't necessarily equal less painful. How was I supposed to know if this stuff would work any better on me? I guess any improvement would be worthwhile, but ultimately isn't it just better not to remember anything about the procedure? That's all I really cared about.

Then the good doctor lit the fuse to the last weapon in his arsenal, and lobbed it at me.

"Have you ever been on nitrous oxide?"

Ka-boom!

"What's that?" I asked.

"Laughing gas," he replied.

First of all, I had no idea that laughing gas was a real thing. I truly thought it only existed in cartoons and movies. I just kept thinking of Steve Martin playing the psychotic dentist in *Little Shop of Horrors* – a character that always made me incredibly uncomfortable, even though I loved Steve Martin. Spoiler alert: in the movie, the dentist straps a tank of "laughing gas" to his back and inhales it until he dies of laughter. I mean, come on. How was I supposed to know this product actually existed in the real world?

"No, I've never been on that," I said.

"Well, we can give you that, too, in addition to the Xanax. It'll make you completely relaxed and adds another layer of anesthetic. You won't feel anything, trust me."

Fascinating. I was beginning to warm up to the idea. Maybe this was all an elaborate ruse, but his sales pitch was working: a new numbing agent that was better than Novocaine, the latest technology in lasers and drills, a Xanax, and this intriguing new 'nitrous oxide'…I was willing to give it a shot.

I made an appointment for the following week to have the cavity filled.

The entire week leading up to the procedure, I had my usual flare of stomach problems, lack of sleep and lack of concentration. As much as I wanted to believe everything the new dentist was promising, I still had a tremendous fear that the drugs wouldn't work and that I'd end up being strapped down by nurses and tortured with dental instruments until my mind cracked.

The culmination of these fears came to a palpable fruition on the day of the appointment.

My procedure was in the afternoon, and as the early hours of the day slowly passed, my anxiety grew. I couldn't eat. My palms were sweaty and my breathing was frantic and shallow.

About twenty minutes before I left my apartment, I made an impulsive last-minute decision. Regardless of whether or not these untested drugs would work on me, I was determined that I would *not* allow myself to feel anything in that dentist's chair.

That meant getting creative with whatever I could dig up around the house.

I found marijuana. I found vodka. I found old painkillers and muscle relaxers.

If this concerns you a little, you are probably a normal functioning human being with a healthy mind and body. If you had no reaction to that combination of drugs being mixed with Xanax and nitrous oxide, you probably have a drug problem.

This was a terrible idea, but at the time it seemed perfectly logical.

I took it all. Not really knowing which, if any, might actually help me. I was desperate and not thinking clearly.

In case you're wondering, the prescription drugs were all legally obtained leftovers from an old injury. The weed was admittedly less legally obtained, but only because New York didn't happen to be one of the states that permitted medical marijuana at the time. (Judge not lest ye be judged.)

By the time I reached the dentist's office, I was higher than Jesus on Easter. Not wanting to blow my cover, I opted to basically not speak to anyone if I could avoid it. Apparently it worked, because none of them seemed to notice how wrecked I was. They must have thought my silence was just how I normally processed my dental anxiety.

I don't remember actually taking the Xanax, but I'm positive that I did. Likewise, I don't remember getting from the waiting room to the procedure room. The first thing I do remember is the laughing gas and the anesthetic injection.

The nitrous oxide mask was already on my face. There was a very faint scent of something sort of fruity, almost like bubble gum, emanating from it. Immediately my anxiety reignited and panic began flaring through my nervous system. My heart was racing; I could feel it pounding hard in my chest. Despite all of the "downer" drugs in my system, my fear was pushing through to the surface. Believe it or not, even on all those substances, I was aware of being too aware. This was the first time in over a decade that I had not been blacked out during a dental procedure, and this caused serious terror.

I reasoned that if the fruity smell was the savior-gas flowing to my nose, and I was still cognizant enough to register it, this nitrous stuff was nowhere close to being as effective as my "forgetting drugs." The notion of possibly enduring a real life nightmare again after so many years of clever and diligent avoidance was unthinkable. Nevertheless, here I was. It was about to happen.

Was it too late to stop all of this? I was about to ask as the doctor sat down next to me and prepared the tools and drills, but I was too stoned and couldn't think quickly or clearly enough to communicate.

After some generic salutation that I could barely make out through all the drugs, the doctor shoved a long cotton swab, covered in pink topical anesthetic, into my mouth and let it sit there for a few seconds. I realized I was gripping the arms of the dental chair so hard that my fingers hurt. My eyes were wide, and I could feel sweat beading on my forehead. Again, I wanted to say something – anything to stall him – but nothing came out.

Helplessly, I watched as he lifted the "Septocaine" needle.

This was it. There was no turning back. I'm awake. I'm aware. I'm unable to speak. I'm going to shit my pants.

Then he looked over to the dental hygienist sitting just on the other side of my fully reclined dental chair.

"Turn it up," he said.

I wondered what that meant. Turn what up?

Instantly, the facemask flooded with an intense burst of fruity smelling gas.

Maybe this was my chance, I thought. If this strong new smell was the gas at full blast, I was going to take advantage of it. I started sucking the nitrous oxide out of the mask with as much force as my lungs could give me. Deep, frenetic gasps, like a drowning man gasping for air. I wanted to drain the NO2 from that machine and fly far, far away.

Dr. Fantastic steadied his hand, removed the cotton swab and made a move like he was going to inject me with the Septocaine. I tensed a little as he made his approach, but then something strange happened.

The needle disappeared into my mouth, along with Dr. Fantastic's hand, wrist, and arm. He had apparently driven his fist right through the back of my head.

I didn't feel anything.

That's when I knew the nitrous oxide was working.

More than being pain-free after having been gored through the neck by a superhero-dentist, I had an overwhelming sensation of comfort about it all.

Then things got even weirder.

As he removed his arm from my head, the nurse, who had been hiding behind me, came out to hand him some instrument while making casual conversation. I saw her crossing from left to right in front of me as the doctor leaned into my face. Suddenly, in mid-sentence, the sound of her voice slowed and became impossibly deep, like a secret witness in a true crime documentary.

As the woman moved back to her seat, she left a trail of what I can only describe as visualized movement behind her, like an infinity mirror. Fractals of her image, splitting over and over as she moved across my line of sight. In addition, her movement was slowing down, just like the sound of her voice. Everything in the room got slower and slower until finally it was all completely still – frozen in time.

My mind was racing trying to make sense of it. Then, suddenly, my body was racing, too.

Perhaps "body" is the wrong word. Although it still looked like my body, I could feel that it wasn't. It was as if my life force had peeled itself away from my physical body and leapt into the air.

Effortlessly, I soared out of the chair, through the roof of the building, out of New York City, higher and higher into the sky until I pushed through the atmosphere and raced into outer space.

I knew only two things in this moment: one, the dental filling was the least of my problems, and two, I was on *way* too many drugs.

Ho. Ly.
Shit.

"For we are the local embodiment of a Cosmos grown to self-awareness. We have begun to contemplate our origins: starstuff pondering the stars."

– Carl Sagan

CHAPTER 6:
THE ABYSS

I was moving so intensely fast that all of the stars and moons and planets in the entire Universe seemed to be flying past me in a massive blur. All of Creation itself – reduced to walls of speeding light all around me.

Perhaps "creation" isn't exactly the right word, seeing as how I'd abandoned the idea of God by this point in my life. Yet, even in that state of mind, it felt less like mere light and matter flying past me and more like...well, *Creation*.

All sense of time was absolutely gone. I could barely maintain any sense of self. It was as if my entire trip to the dentist that day, which I knew on some level was currently in the process of happening, had already begun to feel like an abstract memory – something from my distant past.

I continued speeding along until, finally, I reached the end of space itself, the edge of all things, some great blackness beyond. I was floating in this unnatural silence and stillness that nothing else in the Universe could reach.

There in the darkness, a singular white light appeared, like a beacon.

I drifted towards the light and looked into it. I reached for it, and held it in my outstretched hands.

As I touched it, I could sense that it was not made of atoms or molecules, but rather was some kind of energy outside our perception of matter entirely, if that makes sense. Outside of anything I knew, at least.

A silent voice rose up around me and somehow conveyed to me that this light was a spiritual representation of a life event, one of many such events within the wide range of my existence. This particular event was one about a dentist and a great fear and an unlikely sort of spiritual awakening yet to come.

Still looking into the light, I could see that this moment was enormously important to the course of my life, yet simultaneously it was completely insignificant – a paradox that somehow made perfect sense.

Then another beacon lit up in the blackness next to me. This was yet another critically important life event, which I recognized as a recent job loss that had left me emotionally and financially wrecked.

Beyond that, another beacon appeared. This one was of an overwhelmingly happier time, the day I married my wife (only a few months prior).

Then another beacon, and another, and another appeared, forming a vast timeline that mapped every major event in my life, or rather, in my *existence*. Far down the line of white lights that stretched nearly into infinity, there was one particularly bright spot that I recognized as my birth. The beginning of what I thought was "me." Intriguingly, the long line of events stretched far beyond that point.

This cosmic timeline indicated that I "began" long before my birth, that my existence stretched all the way back to the beginning of all things, in a time before time itself.

If my existence began at the beginning of all things, I wondered where it ended. I looked down the great line of beacons in the opposite direction, into the future.

Somewhere deep in my future's timeline, I saw one particularly bright light that was my death – or, I should say, the death of my body – but the great story of my existence extended far, far beyond that, nearly into eternity.

The weight of this information on my Agnostic mind was overbearing, yet oddly freeing. A pattern of such paradoxes was beginning to emerge.

I turned my attention back towards the light in my hands. This spectacle of dentistry and drugs and fear suddenly seemed so *absurd* in the grand scheme of these cosmic things. What power did this fear really have over me when placed against the magnitude of existence itself, placed against life and death and love and stars and galaxies and eternity? It felt so small, so insignificant, so incredibly weak. This fear of dentistry would last a handful of seconds and minutes in a line of "being" that stretched on for eons! If everything I was seeing was true, my spirit had witnessed the formation of suns and planets and civilizations, and here I was panicking, clinging onto the arms of a dentist chair on the Upper East Side…for what?

The absurdity of it became irrepressible and I began to laugh. It started as a sort of modest chuckle. Then, it grew. I released the light from my hands and my body drifted away until I could see the full vastness of the timeline before me.

I was filled with a deep-rooted joy as I began to understand the length and scope of my own story in the Universe.

The laughter became uncontrollable.

The further back I drifted, the more I became aware and the harder I laughed. I became so lost in the irony of it all – in the majesty and the infinity of it all – that my laughter blossomed into something I had never heard before. It was as if my soul itself was laughing. The distorted sounds were an odd clashing between the body and the spirit, as if my spirit were trying to use my vocal cords as a translator, but the voice box couldn't handle the signal or something, so all that came out was a strange, ecstatic bellowing.

Eventually, the laughter dissipated, the beacons dimmed and suddenly, in a bright flash of swirling light, I fell, rushing back towards the earth. Suns and planets became flashes of crane lights and wall-mounted televisions…dental instruments buzzed in distant echoes…the sounds of familiar voices flickered and were gone, quickly replaced by a gentle rumbling all around.

All went dark. There was a strange noise, like giant stones scraping against each other. It was as if I had been pulled not just back to the earth's surface, but through it. As if I went straight through the dental chair, then deep into the core of the planet.

I opened my eyes.

A strange new world had emerged around me, and suddenly, I forgot everything about the dentist, the beacons of light at the edge of the Universe, and anything else that may have been informing my sense of reality.

A twilight sky hung overhead, fading from dark orange and purple into black. I was standing on some sort of foreign landscape, like an alien planet in a sci-fi movie, or a Dali painting.

I found myself walking slowly along the strange desert terrain, painfully bewildered. Where was I? And how did I get here?

At first, I thought I was controlling my own pace and movement, but I soon realized I was not. My legs were moving on their own, and the rest of me was just along for the ride.

I didn't have much time to take any of this in before I saw a terror in the distance. A giant hole – a mass of blackness that stretched all the way to the distant horizon – and I was walking straight toward it.

I kept telling my legs to stop, to turn back before I got any closer, but it was no use. I marched on, helplessly.

As I got closer and closer, I saw the jagged edges of this giant cliff, stretching out in both directions almost as far as my eyes could see. It was so wide and deep that it could have swallowed the moon whole and still had room for more.

There was no bottom to it, no end, just an immeasurable pit.

I was terrified, utterly terrified, of what was about to happen.

I looked around frantically for something to hold on to – a stone, a root, anything – but there was nothing.

With only a few strides left, my legs pulled me towards the abyss in slow motion, so that I had ample time to absorb my fate.

"Maybe," I thought, "maybe this is just a dream, and when I fall I'll wake-up before I hit the bottom." But something deep inside me knew that this would not be the case.

My body lurched forward into the great nothingness and I looked down and saw my foot leaving the last bit of earth beneath it.

My stomach rose into my throat as the air in front of me began to press against my face. Without a sound, I felt a voice all around me and I understood. This vast abyss before me was my subconscious, and I was about to plummet into it. I knew this would be a place where unresolved emotions, conflicts and fears ran amok – a place of dreams and nightmares. Anything could be waiting for me down there.

Without warning, the chains of my suspended animation were cut loose, and like Alice down the rabbit hole, I dropped.

Rapidly, I descended, fighting and clawing at the dark around me. I let out a piercing howl as the terror of the fall overcame me.

Down and down and down, I twisted and spun. The sound of the air whipping over me was deafening.

I fell for so long that the dim light from the world above became a tiny speck, and disappeared. I was surrounded by this dark, speeding emptiness.

I have no way of telling how long I descended. It felt like hours, perhaps days – long enough that I began to hope for the bottom, just to end the fall.

And then, finally...

There was an ear-splitting silence. The sound of the whipping wind had stopped.

I pressed my fingers out in front of me, and sure enough, there was something there. Not ground or rock, but just a sort of plane.

I pushed myself up, onto my feet.

This was it. The bottom. I was deep inside myself, utterly alone. It was a menacing, soul-consuming solitude.

I looked up from where I had fallen, and there was nothing.

I looked behind me, into the darkness, and there was nothing, not even the slightest hint of shape or substance.

I turned forward again, then staggered back as I saw Him.

Standing not two feet in front of my face, His eyes piercing through me, His visage stern and His entire body coursing with a palpable energy that illuminated Him against the stifling darkness.

He was epic and devastating. His presence pulled all of the air from my lungs. I gasped and fell to my knees.

I was standing face to face with God.

"THE FEAR OF THE LORD IS
THE BEGINNING OF KNOWLEDGE."

— PROVERBS 1:7

CHAPTER 7:
JUDGEMENT DAY

I was dead.

In that moment, I knew I had overdosed. With all of the downers in my system, my heart rate must have reached a critic low and simply stopped beating, or the muscles around my lungs had become so weak that they could no longer import oxygen. This was the end.

It was the only thing that made any sense as I cowered in front of the Creator of the Universe.

He didn't have to explain to me who He was, I already knew. I can't explain how I knew, I just did.

The fact that He was standing in front of me now was terrifying because up until a second ago, I didn't even believe He existed.

If judgment day had come for me, I was totally fucked. I wasn't a believer. (And I used words like "fucked.") I had obviously failed the test of life and arrived at all the wrong conclusions, and now I was going to pay the ultimate price for that mistake. God's wrath.

I saw a fire burning in God's eyes – a "righteous anger," as Christians like to call it. His mouth began to open. A vacuum of air seemed to funnel past me. He was either about to speak or He was about to vaporize me with some kind of holy hellfire, like a dragon incinerating an unworthy knight.

Lucky for me, a voice, not fire, bellowed forth.

It had a booming quality like thunder that rumbled and crashed as He spoke. There was a gravitas to it that truly felt powerful enough to have called the stars into existence, and no part of my cynical mind questioned

His authority.

"*STOP TELLING PEOPLE I DON'T EXIST,*" He roared.

Oh. My. God.
Literally.
The words ripped from His lips and seemed to whip across my body.

He had not spoken in English, mind you, but in some kind of spiritual language that I understood perfectly. It was wondrous and bizarre.

His fiery eyes bore down on me as I cowered before Him.

It seems strange to think of myself, a grown man, shaking with fear at the sight of something so abstractly conjured. Perhaps this was all standard fare for veteran hallucinogenic drug trippers, but it was an unexpected and unfamiliar experience for me.

Granted, I wasn't entirely myself in the context of all this. I was a different version of myself. It was me, but without any of the judgmental or cynical chatter that normally buzzes around my mind. It was the most fragile part of my ego, alone, separated from the whole, stripped of all its defenses and utterly exposed. This raw nakedness was the only sense of myself that I could grasp in the moment.

We sat in pregnant silence, as if He were waiting for me to answer for my crimes. Slowly, I opened my eyes and looked up at Him. I stuttered and choked as I tried to speak.

"I didn't know you existed," I stammered.

"Others may have that excuse, but you do not," He said plainly. "You have always known of my existence. You are angry that I am not more accessible to you, so you deny me and you deny yourself, claiming things you know are false. Has denying my existence made life more bearable for you? Has it made you either happy or wise? No. It has made you lost."

His words were ego shattering. He was right.

I guess it's hard to argue with God. He clearly seemed to know me better than I knew myself. Deep inside, I did always believe that there was something out there. I wanted to believe – even if my intellect rejected it. I envied others who found such faith and were content not to question it.

I knew from having watched enough episodes of *Law & Order* that defendants were almost never encouraged to testify voluntarily at their own trial. Nevertheless, I took the stand, and feebly tried to explain myself while not seeming too defensive or impudent.

"I needed proof," I said. "There was no proof of your existence. I understand the idea of 'faith' – that it's not about hard evidence. But even in the Bible, when Thomas doubted Jesus's resurrection, God showed Himself to Thomas and let him put his fingers in Jesus's wounds. He gave Thomas proof! He gave all of the disciples proof, hard evidence that Jesus had returned from the dead. If hard evidence was necessary for them, why isn't it necessary for the rest of us? Why are we told to forget about our insatiable need for proof? In all other aspects of our lives, we rely on tangible evidence to make decisions. You created us that way. Why, then, are we expected to accept and understand the spiritual world without any hard evidence to support it? And what's more, how can you come at the end of my life to judge me for being confused by it all?"

Almost assuming a human tone, He replied, "I have not come to judge you."

"You haven't?" I asked, genuinely surprised. "I'm not dead?"

"You are not dead," He answered, partly amused.

Then He corrected my example about Thomas and the disciples. He explained that almost everything I knew about Christ and his early followers was either skewed or completely inaccurate. Apparently Thomas was not given proof of Jesus's resurrection in the way that the Bible tells it. Nonetheless, even if you take the Bible stories at face value, Thomas was given proof at the precise moment that he needed it, so that he could believe. Likewise, God told me, He was appearing to me now, at this precise moment, so that I could believe.

It may be true that those who can "believe without seeing" are blessed (according to the Bible[6]), but that does not mean that all those who *must see* in order to believe are necessarily lost…they simply walk a different path. This is what God told me.

Despite hearing these words and being filled with a sort of inner "rightness," a sense of powerful truth, my inner skeptic was released from wherever it had been sequestered and slowly crept to the surface.

I wanted to believe what He was saying, but was this "God" really the "proof" I needed in order to believe in Him again? Was this even really God?

Some part of me was still anchored in reality. Let's keep it real: *I was on drugs.*

I began to suspect that I had some power here. This was, after all, my subconscious, wasn't it? Didn't that give me some inherent right to question these visions? Call it a home-field advantage.

"How can I be sure you're really God?" I asked. "How do I know you're not just a figment of my imagination, brought to life by the drugs

I'm on?" ("A blot of mustard, a crumb of cheese..." Charles Dickens, anyone?)

Without hesitation, God went to work...almost as if He had done all of this many times before.

He offered to demonstrate His God-ness to me in two ways. The first was a demonstration of his ability to manipulate the physical world, to show His command over the laws of nature. The second was to answer every question about Himself or about the Universe that I could think to ask.

That was one hell of an offer, I thought.

But before I could leap on it, as I *obviously* wanted to do, He gave me a warning. He said that these demonstrations would still not make me believe. Not because I was so flawed, but because believing is just so difficult. No amount of miracles or divine knowledge can quell all doubt, because doubt is a necessary component of faith. This relationship between faith and doubt was constructed by design, He told me.

Nonetheless, faith of any kind requires a certain proverbial leap, and some of us are simply willing to leap farther than others.

In my mind's eye, God's words came to life. I could *see* everything He was describing.

I saw a great chasm between two cliffs; one cliff was Logic and the other was Faith. In the distance, the land connected, revealing that although the two cliffs appeared to be separate, they were in fact one. There were three lines of people crossing in various ways from one side to the other. No matter which line you were in, the cliff of Logic acted as a sort of springboard over the gulf; in order to reach Faith, you had to have a running start on Logic. Some people could make incredibly large leaps with virtually no use of Logic at all. And so they stayed and jumped from the farthest point between the two cliffs. Others, like myself, required a mountain of Logic before taking the leap. These people jumped from a much more shallow distance between the two. Still others, even more skeptical than I, refused to jump at all. They would insist that the shores of Logic reach the shores of Faith completely before stepping over.

There was no inherent judgment over which group of people were better or worse. There was no special reward for jumping further, no punishment for not jumping at all. Every path over the divide was divine in its own right.

When these images concluded, God knelt down to where I was sitting. He looked into my eyes and I could feel a weighted sense of empathy in Him.

"If you are ready?" He asked. I nodded that I was. "You must trust me, no matter what you see."

That sounded ominous, but I nodded again, cueing Him to proceed with His demonstration.

"Tell me what you need to see in order to believe," He commanded rather majestically.

"If I'm being honest," I said, "you'd have to show me a lot. Move a mountain, or turn me into a giant taller than New York's skyscrapers, or create a new galaxy! If we're really doing this, I think I need to see something epic."

He nodded stoically, again as if He had done all this before.

Then, I could sense something dark growing within the link that He and I shared. It was a sense of foreboding that is hard to explain.

Without a word, the image of God slowly faded until He disappeared completely.

Something deep within me became tense. I was alone again in the abyss, suddenly stung by an unshakable premonition that something monstrous was looming in the darkness around me. I felt it clawing at me, though I could not yet see what it was.

The air became foul.

I felt like I was suffocating, as if someone had me by the throat.

My mouth dropped open and I began gasping, but it was too late...the demonstration had begun.

My eyes shot open.

The light of the craning dental lamp was blinding, and every noise in the office, mechanical and human alike, was a bombardment to my senses. Every sight and sound in the room was overwhelmingly articulated.

I was hyper-aware of everything, as if there were no drugs in my system at all. Given my surroundings, my phobia rose up from my chest with its talons and razor-like teeth gleaming. It devoured me whole.

Both Dr. Fantastic and his assistant were busy at work. He had just finished drilling part of the tooth, and had begun changing the drill head from a larger bit to a finer one, or some other horrible thing that I didn't want to witness.

The hygienist was aiming the suction device at my cheeks and gums. It had a translucent tube through which I could see it wasn't just removing saliva. It was also vacuuming up blood, which naturally relaxed me enough to have an acute panic attack.

There was a bite block in my mouth forcing my jaw open, the exact same kind I remembered from my childhood.

I could feel God's presence. It was not the merciful presence that people often associate with that phrase. No, this was a cold and terrifying presence, not a God of comfort or love, but a God of wrath.

"You want to see proof of my power?" I heard His thoughts. "Close your eyes."

Anxiously, I tried to close my eyes, eager to blot out all of the horrifying images I was seeing…but I couldn't. My eyelids felt weirdly heavy, weighed down in the wrong direction, keeping my eyes wide open.

God's voice continued, "You can't close them because I'm holding them open. I allow or disallow every breath you take, every heartbeat, every fiber of every muscle, every cell within you answers to me. If you need to *see* in order to believe, your eyes must stay *open*."

As panic set in, my eyes began to burn, exposed to the dry winter air. Still, they stayed open.

I desperately wanted to beg for mercy and to somehow stop this from going any further, but it was as if my thoughts themselves had been muzzled. This was one of the most frightening and invasive sensations of all – the mind itself being muted against its will.

In this horrifying state, God explained to me that the first phase of every man's journey to God is *fear*.

Like anything in nature – fire, water, wind, earth – you cannot truly comprehend the power of a God without first fearing it, humbled by the sheer magnitude of its strength over you. It is not an irrational fear based on mythology or moral ideology, it is a simple, practical fear based on the nature of God's vastness over the smallness of Man.

Just as I saw the doctor finish assembling the tiny drill head and position the instrument on my tooth, everything in the room abruptly became motionless – the doctor, the hygienist, the television in the background, everything stood in complete stillness – an eerie stop.

The sounds of the room, likewise, became suspended in a sort of infinite reverberating loop. After only a moment of this awful noise, it became an assault on my ears and mind.

In this unnatural, suspended state, God explained what was about to happen.

By controlling time, God could cast me into my own personal Hell. The dentist was about to hit a nerve in my tooth, God told me in no uncertain terms, just milliseconds from now. God was about to suspend me in that pain – indefinitely.

It didn't matter now that my thoughts had been supernaturally muted; my mind was silent, paralyzed by fear.

This was the pain I feared above all else and had spent years of my life escaping. And here I was, facing an inescapable torment, so that I might come to understand that the God in my head was who He claimed to be.

"Time is irrelevant to me," He said. "How long will it take for you to believe in my power over you?"

There are no words that can describe the unmitigated terror I was experiencing in this moment. I mean that literally: the fear was so overwhelming that there are no words in any earthly language that can express it. I say this with authority not because I know all the languages ever spoken, but because the fear was not a natural fear. It was some kind of spiritual, *super*natural fear – an otherworldly terror. The vocabulary of our species is simply incapable of describing it. That is the level of profound duress I was in in that moment, and it is precisely where God wanted me to be.

I suppose the one thing I instantly came to terms with was what it meant to know "the fear of God."

As a teenager growing up in the Church, I had always assumed that I understood the Old Testament references to God's wrath, as well as the New Testament passages about "the fear of God." Yet, I realized in this moment that I had never truly understood. It was so much easier to focus on the gentle aspects of God that make up the tenets of modern Christianity – God the protector, the savior, the steward of kindness, mercy and love. In other words, this was an entirely new dimension of God that was, until now, purely theoretical.

"How long will it take for you to see the truth?" He asked.

Suddenly my thoughts were unleashed and permitted to assert themselves. My mind began spewing a fountain of emotional pleading.

"I believe you! I see the truth! I understand. You don't need to show me anymore, please; I believe you, I believe you, I *believe*!"

All at once, the relentless reverse-gravity sensation around my eyes released and my eyelids slammed shut. The echoing loop of suspended dental office clatter was silenced. I was once again alone with God in the safety of my black, subconscious pit.

I felt weak, shell-shocked from the suspended reality. I didn't want to move or speak or think. It was as if my soul itself had become fatigued.

God knelt down beside me again to look me in the eyes. His voice was soft and steady now. He told me that this entire episode had only been a demonstration, and that He never would have harmed me.

I just looked at Him for several seconds, trying to read His face as if He were human.

"But you just told me to fear you," I said.

"I told you that in order to understand me, you must first understand my true power," He replied. "In your earthly body, this can only come through the knowledge of fear."

He told me that fear is the first gate through which all men must pass in order to truly know God. Many try to reach Him without fear, and they fail. Through this terrifying example, I had just passed through the gate. Now my understanding of God could begin.

"This was only meant to awaken you," He said, "to test you, as you have tested me. You were never in danger. I am not a god of torment or punishment."

"But...what if I hadn't believed so quickly?" I asked.

God smiled, as if to say that He knew how I was going to respond all along.

"It was your fear of that pain that brought me here," He said. "I came to protect you from it, not to torture you with it."

Now I understood what He meant to teach me. God's power is not found in the moving of mountains; God's power is so great that it can be found in the mere blinking of an eye.

This, in a nutshell, sums up much of humanity's problem with faith. Our expectations of God are disproportionate.

I overshot, asking Him to turn me into Godzilla or to build me a constellation in order to prove Himself – but then again, who wouldn't?

He scared the shit out of me, but I guess that was all part of His plan. Who was I to judge Him for His tactics? "The Lord works in mysterious ways," right?

"So...now what?" I asked.

"What would you like to know?" He replied.

"Religion is belief in someone else's experience. Spirituality is having your own experience."

— Deepak Chopra

CHAPTER 8:
QUESTIONS, ANSWERS

PART I: THE LOOKING GLASS

Whenever I've shared this experience with anyone, their first question is almost always, "What did God look like?"

Ironically, for reasons I can't explain, it wasn't until this moment that I began to really take in God's physical appearance.

Granted, as soon as I had encountered Him I knew exactly who He was. His appearance was somewhat irrelevant, in a strange way. Nevertheless, the only explanation I can think of as to why I didn't notice His features before this moment is that, perhaps, He simply didn't want me to.

Either way, as I began to study His face, I recognized that it was…extremely familiar.

There is no easy way to say it, so I'm just going to put it out there: He looked exactly like *me*.

The sublime irony of this was not lost on me. When I asked him why He looked like this, He just smiled and explained that He had no physical form, but that whatever image I was seeing was one of my own choosing. Apparently, His natural form, if you can call it that, is so otherworldly that the human brain literally can't see it. In order to make sense of His appearance, people's brains automatically select an image, subconsciously, and apply it to Him. He told me this is why there are so many differing accounts of His physical appearance throughout history (including multiple contrasting accounts in the Bible).

Nonetheless, I protested. Why on Earth would I have chosen for God to look like a mirror image of myself?? It felt a bit egocentric, even for me.

His response still haunts me, even now.

"Because you needed to see me in a form that you knew you could trust. And you don't trust anyone but yourself," He said.

It felt like a bomb had detonated in my chest. It was an incredibly difficult thing for me to hear, especially at that point in my life. I had just gotten married a few months earlier. I had an active relationship with both my parents and my two siblings. I had literally hundreds of happy acquaintances and a handful of very close friends. Yet, here I was, with a God manifested in my own image, telling me that I was incapable of trusting any of them.

It took years to fully understand why I had become so completely self-reliant – years of therapy and self-exploration. The important thing though, for the sake of this story, is that I knew He was right.

The truth of His words was crushing. I always felt strongest, safest and most efficient when I was alone. I did not easily forge emotional connections with others. It was far easier to keep everyone, even my closest friends and loved ones, at a safe distance. That way, when they inevitably let me down, the risks to my well-being were minimal. This pattern of emotional detachment felt utterly exposed now, called out by God Himself.

I sat there for some time, looking over the wrinkles and folds of my own face as they were reflected back to me through the face of God.

Eventually, I turned to Him and asked what He *was*, exactly. If my mind had just "assigned" Him a physical form in order for me to process His presence, what was behind the mirage?

I theorized that He was possibly made of light, or pure energy, or even "dark matter," whatever that is. But He rejected all of those things and said, "I am nothing that you can comprehend in your earthly form. I simply *am*."

I understood what He was saying on a conceptual level, but nonetheless this seemed like a cop-out, a deflection. 'The answer is that you can't comprehend the answer.' It sort of defeats the purpose of asking questions, doesn't it?

So I protested a bit and He went on to explain that He would happily show me the answers to any of life's riddles, but that some of those answers would be incomprehensible for one of two reasons: one, the information simply wasn't compatible with my brain (for example, His physical appearance), or two, possession of certain information would destroy some part of my destiny (i.e., knowing the future). It wasn't that these answers were off-limits, necessarily. He was willing to show them to me regardless, but He told me that it would be pointless because I would not be able to take those kinds of answers with me back into the physical world.

I've watched a lot of *Star Trek* over the years, so God's concerns about the space-time continuum made perfect sense to me. Obviously, if I knew the circumstances of my own death, for instance, I'd instinctively avoid it and ruin the natural timeline of the Universe. Far be it from me to want to do that.

However, the "your brain is too small" argument did not sit well with me. It's an old Christian apologetics trick that I was familiar with from growing up. I always considered it a cheap defense tactic Christians used as a last resort to justify why they didn't have to actually answer tough questions about God. "Well, God's just too complicated for mere humans to understand. It would be like a human trying to explain algebra to a cockroach!" (There is a quote from the Old Testament book of Ecclesiastes – my favorite book in the Bible, FYI – that says mankind cannot fully understand "the ways of God."[7] So it's not that modern Christians created this weak logic loophole, the Bible actually backs it up.)

All of this to say, the God in my head wasn't really saying anything that was totally surprising or contradictory to my previously ingrained theological beliefs.

God did, however, explain this basic apologetics tactic in a way that I could empathize with. He essentially broke it down for me on a technical level, suggesting that our brains are sort of like computer hard drives; they have a finite amount of storage space and operate on a specific operating system. Trying to explain certain things to me (or any human) would be like trying to install Microsoft software from the year 2150 onto a 1984 Macintosh. It wasn't ideological; it was just a raw hardware problem. Being a novice tech geek, this line of reasoning seemed to checked out. (Admittedly, though, God created that hardware problem on purpose for reasons I will discuss later.)

You can also compare this phenomenon to the capabilities of the human eye. Our eyes can only perceive a small fraction of the actual light spectrum that exists in the Universe. By asking to see God's natural form, I was asking to see something that my eyes were literally incapable of seeing (like infrared or x-ray light).

Nonetheless, I was feisty and wanted more, so I asked Him to show me what He looked like anyway.

I am nothing if not persistent.

Again, God smiled. Then He revealed to me His true form.

Wouldn't you know it, He was right! I can't remember a damn thing about what He "truly" looked like. Whatever He showed me, I was unable to grasp it or retain it. Back to my computer analogy: you might say He overrode my programming and dropped a .dmg file right onto my Windows desktop. Even now, I can see the file, but there's no way to open it. (Yes, like you, I am astounded by my own geekery.)

Regardless, I felt somehow satisfied that He had kept up His end of the bargain, cop-out or not. He withheld nothing from me for the rest of my epic journey with Him, despite the fact that most of it, perhaps 70-80% if I had to take a guess, was completely beyond my cosmic pay-grade.

He did, however, give me one reassuring consolation. He promised that one day, after my death, when my soul was no longer bound by earthly limitations, I would remember everything He had shown me. So the full extent of my vision may not have been completely in vain. It will just be a few years before I'll have access to those memories again. Here's hoping!

Luckily, though, there were many answers and cosmic visions that my limited monkey-brain *was* capable of grasping. I say "luckily" because otherwise, this book would probably have ended right about…here.

PART II: I AM

Since we were just getting to know each other, it seemed natural to start with the basics. I asked God if He had a name…you know, besides just "God."

He told me that He went by many names. "Too many to count."

I knew from my boyhood study of the scriptures that many names had been ascribed to God: "Adonai," the simple prefix "El" (as in "El Shaddai" and others), the vowel-less "YHWH" (typically written/spoken as "Yahweh" or "Jehovah"), and so on. This is to say nothing of the dozens – perhaps even hundreds – of titles and adjectives that are used as Godly appellations in the Bible.

Nonetheless, I pushed him for a "real name," as I so crudely put it. Perhaps a name that He thought fit Him best. I was particularly interested in His own sense of identity, rather than the identity that other people had cast upon Him over the ages.

He became almost defensive in His response. He said that all of the names people had ascribed to Him were equally "real."

To articulate this, He pointed out that in most cultures today, people have multiple names. They have a first name, a middle and a last. Some have an additional family name to represent both the maternal and paternal bloodlines. Some take on a married name. There are religious names, such as a Hebrew name in Judaism, or a confirmation name in Catholicism. Then there are nicknames and pet names, of which a person may have an unlimited number, as well as aliases like pen names, stage names, Internet handles, etc. Many people have titles ranging from a simple Mister or Missus to the merited Reverend, Doctor, Esquire, etc. Still further out on the branches of human identity are number systems like social security numbers, birthdays, uniform numbers (sports players and police officers, for example), credit card numbers, etc. The list is endless.

While none of these "names" can capture the entirety of who a person is, each one has its unique place within humanity's complex identification system. We respond to all of these names and titles and aliases whenever it suits us to do so. Likewise, God has a vast number of epithets, each with its unique place within *His* complex identity.

At first, I wasn't particularly interested in any of His names that fell outside the Judeo-Christian tradition. But it was beginning to dawn on me that He wasn't just referring to His various Biblical names. He seemed to be implying that He was not only the God of Christianity/Judaism, but the God of...well, everything.

I asked Him if that were true, if He was the universal "Creator" at the root of every religion. His response was concise, though He seemed to sort of shrug the question off.

He said, "I am what I am. I created all things, and there are no other creators besides me."

I'm still not sure which is theoretically worse, discovering that the God from your childhood actually exists, or discovering that all of the Gods in the history of humanity actually exist.

Needless to say, as an Agnostic at the time, this was all pretty epic.

It seemed like a victory for monotheists everywhere until He went on to clarify that He was neither a singular god, nor plural. He also claimed to be neither male nor female. He was beyond such things. As He kept saying, He simply "was."

Despite the fact that humans tended to dislike paradox, the Universe was fraught with it, because the Universe was modeled after God Himself. Therefore, God was never plainly black or white, right or wrong, this or that: He was always both.

The answer was never "yes or no," but always "yes *and* no."

In this way, God was both the narrow, isolated God of Christianity as well as the broad, unified Creator that encompassed all faith traditions.

How was this paradox possible? How could the God of Christianity be the same God of Islam, and Hinduism, and Paganism?

Having grown up in the South, I knew all too well that it would be blasphemy to suggest that God was "universal" and that He somehow transcended the Bible and/or the Church. It was a seemingly heretical surprise, then, when God explained that He spoke in many tongues (or spiritual languages) so that all men could hear His voice.

I asked why He didn't just speak to everyone in the same spiritual language, and He said it was because He was too complex for that. Likewise, human beings (who were crafted in His image) were intentionally designed with a similar capacity for complexity. A one-size-fits-all communication with Him would have reduced mankind's capacity for understanding the beauty of God through diversity and wonderment.

I'm butchering this, but essentially He said this: "I am the entire spectrum of existence, Alpha to Omega. I am the shepherd of the entire world and not one of my flock can stray so far that they cannot be found. None are lost, even in the seemingly darkest of places, I am there."

As He spoke, I saw a vision – like a parable – flickering across the backs of my eyelids.

It was the pitch black of night. A man wandered too far from his camp and became lost in a dense forest. He stumbled in the dark and began to fall. He reached out for anything to hold on to, and just then, God's right hand appeared and guided him back to the light of his campfire. When the man was safe, he turned to look at God in the light, but God had already gone. His work was done.

Elsewhere, a woman was lost in the same dark wilderness. She too stumbled and reached out for anything to save her from falling. Then, God's left hand appeared and guided her back to the light of her campfire. When she too turned to look at God, He was gone.

The next day, the man began to preach all around the forest that he had met God, and that God was a Right Hand. Meanwhile, the woman began to preach all around the forest that she had encountered God, and that God was a Left Hand. Both spoke the truth of how God had revealed Himself to them.

It did not matter to God which of His hands were taken in the darkness, only that each man and woman found their path back to the light.

I realized that because God was vastly more complex than we were capable of fully understanding, He revealed Himself to some of us as a singular god (Christians, Muslims, Jews, etc.) while revealing Himself to others in the form of multiple gods (Hindus, Greeks, Romans, Egyptians, etc.). More fascinating still, God told me that for some people, He revealed Himself as no God at all – instead, He appeared as a sort of "non-God," like nature, or even science, or simply as philosophy itself. Therefore, even Atheists and Humanists were all part of God's vast identity.

For some people, God needed to play the part of the authoritarian who provides order to chaos and sets parameters for goodness and wickedness, so He does. Others need Him to be more abstract; they find divinity through the powers of humanity or through the cosmos – awesome and majestic in their sheer size and intricacy – so, for them, He is that.

"I am the sunrise, and I am the night. I am the God of your forefathers and the knowledge of your grandchildren. I am wisdom itself. I am energy, I am light. I am love. I am war and I am peace. I am the water and the fire. I am life and I am death. I am time itself; I am the beginning and the end. I am all there ever was and all there ever will be. I am nameless, yet have more names than can be counted. I simply *am*. To understand this is to understand the nature of God."

There are many good analogies for the infinite diversity of God. One is to look at faith in the same way we look at language.

Every language has its own methodology. Some languages are derivatives of other languages (for example, French, Spanish, Italian, etc. all stem from Latin), and some languages differ in origin so dramatically that they seem completely incompatible with one another (as English is to Chinese). Yet, every language has the same function: to give people the power to understand their neighbors.

Likewise, every religion is a "spiritual language," each with its own methodology. Some religions are derivatives of other religions (for example, Christianity, Islam, Mormonism, etc., all stem from Judaism). Some religions differ in origin so dramatically that they are seemingly incompatible with one another (as Atheism is to Christian Science). Yet, every religion has the same function: to give people the power to understand their Creator.

While language is a part of a person's identity, no one is defined solely by their language. Likewise, every "spiritual language" is a part of God's identity, but He is not wholly defined by any one of them.

You might also consider that when humans see a rainbow, each color appears unique and separate from the colors around it. But in actuality, all the colors are connected as one unified spectrum of light. Any color can be separated out from the others and viewed in isolation, but this is not the natural order of things. In nature, it's all one.

These patterns of ultimate unification are everywhere throughout our Universe, like repeating fractals. This is because they are all patterned after God, who is equally diverse yet singular.

Despite the universal wisdom I perceived in all of this, I was too preoccupied with my own egocentric baggage to be overly concerned with humanity as a whole.

"If all of this is true," I thought, "then why was God so mad at me for telling people that He didn't exist? After all, if Agnosticism was just part of His vast identity, why couldn't I just be Agnostic?"

Eerily, I didn't have to ask Him. He just responded to the question without prompting.

"That is not your path," He said.

Then He proceeded to chastise me, saying that my spirit had not led me to Agnosticism, but that my disappointment had.

Again, He was right. I felt it even then. I was disappointed in so many of the hands life had recently dealt me, and I had become spiritually lost. I had become bitter.

I was newly married, had a supportive family, money enough to live comfortably, friends who considered me successful. Looking back, I think the truth was that I felt guilty for having all of that, and yet, felt so emotionally and spiritually defeated. I felt ungrateful and weak, so I buried those feelings as best I could and refused to confront them.

The fact that God had called me out both mystified and irritated me.

"Not my path?" I said impetuously. "What path am I supposed to be on?"

God smiled. "The path you're on," He said.

Ugh.

In the end, despite my growing frustrations with His paradoxes, I learned that where we humans hear one brief musical tone that rings out alone in the darkness, God hears an entire symphony, sweeping into eternity. The Universe – with all its stars and planets – is the orchestra. Every man and woman plays their note in the time they are given. Every faith is a harmonious melody. Every generation has its own refrain. And God, the vast and mysterious "*I Am,*" is the song we are all playing.

He might not have a name, but whatever He was, I was beginning to believe.

PART III: The God Particle

Like most objective observers, I was daunted by the mind-numbing cosmic questions surrounding the origins of the Universe and the time preceding the Big Bang. Well, there's no better time to get to the bottom of it than when you're sitting alone in your subconscious with the Creator of said Universe.

The first thing God did was to repeat a phrase He had used before, one that I had heard quoted many times in my youth. He said, "As it is written, I am the beginning and the end."

For many people, those sacred words are meant to imply that God has no beginning and that He will have no end. However, according to the God in my head, this was not the meaning He intended.

The reason this phrase is often used by Christians to answer the question of God's theoretical lifespan is that there are no other explanations offered in the Bible to solve this riddle.

When we talk about "the Big Bang" and the early Universe, it's a weird hypocrisy that some religious folks cannot accept the idea that the Universe just *always* existed. Instead, they insist that it must have originated from something – presumably God. But then you ask them where God came from, and they tell you that God just *always* existed. Doh!

Whether you believe that the Universe always existed or that God always existed, you're stuck with the same conundrum...how does anything exist without a beginning?

Naturally, I asked God this very question.

He told me that He meant His words literally, that He was the alpha and the omega, the beginning and the end. That is, He began the Universe and He will end it. Given that the Universe is made up of nothing but His own thoughts, materialized from nothingness by His own wants,

He literally *was* the Universe. Therefore, when He began, the Universe began. And when He ends, the Universe will end.

Whew.

My head seemed to itch from the inside out trying to wrap my mind around it.

"So…you're going to die someday?" I asked.

He smiled and said, "Dying and ending are not the same thing. I cannot die."

He told me that dying was the result of the process of living – birth, growth, decay and death – a process that He was not, strictly speaking, subject to.

"I was not born, I do not grow old or decay, and I will not die," He said. "I am neither alive nor dead; I simply *am*."

Still, what did it mean for God to have a beginning and an end?

As soon as I thought this, God dawned a sly grin.

"I will show you," He said.

Before my eyes even had a chance to widen, we were speeding off through time and space. In an instant, my body merged into God's and we both seemed to dematerialize.

I was now some kind of observer in an infinite, empty blackness. It was visually identical to the dense black walls of my subconscious, which makes it hard for me to explain how I knew I was in a completely different place and time (er, non-time), but somehow I did.

God was no longer communicating in the spoken language that He had been using, but instead, I could feel His thoughts as if they were my own. It was like I was inside His mind, seeing through His eyes. That's when I realized that what I was watching was not just a demonstration. He was showing me a memory, letting me live through it as if it were my own.

Unlike my actual memories, which fade and crack over time like old photographs, the following events were crystal clear and perfect down to the smallest detail. If I didn't instinctively know that I was somehow channeling God's pre-primordial past, I would have assumed I was witnessing these things in real time.

This was the place of God's beginning, a time before the Universe existed, before "the bang," before anything at all.

At first, I felt nothing. I saw nothing. I was nothing – a mute, motionless, formless state of non-consciousness. Even this dull sense of awareness that I'm describing has been superimposed; in the moment, it was devoid of any thought or sensation at all.

Then, suddenly, the spark of consciousness erupted in me, as if my eyes had opened for the very first time.

It is very difficult to describe what happened next.

I was a tiny spec floating in the vast, empty void. Until this moment, I had apparently been a single particle careening lifelessly through empty space. But now I had collided with another particle and our combined energies formed a kind of molecular consciousness.

We were two separate particles that existed alone and unaware until this moment. But now, because we were together, we were aware. We had a single voice, a single unified thought. (This felt like the first meeting of God and Wisdom, before either had such names, if that makes sense.)

It was at this moment that I could feel my divine inner-self awakening to a powerful sense of free will and almost...a purpose.

I could feel a task of epic proportion teetering towards me, like an unseen horizon out in the darkness. Like I had awakened from an impossibly deep sleep and had to choose to either close my eyes and return to my silent slumber, or to throw off the covers, stand in the darkness and prepare to face the rising of some unknown sun.

Without a moment's hesitation, I chose to rise, and the great journey of Creation had begun, not with an enormous cosmic explosion, but with a small, quiet inhalation.

I examined myself. I appeared to be relatively insignificant; a grayish-blue bubble of cosmic dust without much form or apparent function.

I examined my surroundings. I was alone in a cold, dark, empty vacuum – no stars, no planets, no light or sound – nothing at all.

"What am I?" I could hear myself thinking in a strange voice that was not entirely my own.

The question sparked a chain reaction of lightning fast revelations in my miniature God-mind.

If there was nothing else in the Universe except me, that meant that I was, in essence, the entirety of the Universe.

But what if I were not alone? What if there were another molecule like me? I imagined it.

Instantly, another molecule identical to me, materialized.

My thoughts, I discovered, were capable of materializing. Solely through my imagination, I knew the power of Creation pulsed within me.

I studied my newly created molecule. I searched deep within it and realized that I could pass through it. My consciousness was not bound by physical form, because "matter" (as we call it) was merely an extension of myself. I *was* the matter just as much as I *was* the consciousness that observed it.

I hovered formlessly outside of the two molecules (my original vessel and the twin I had created) and I realized that neither of these molecules were sentient, as I was. I realized that I was still alone.

In a frenzied flood of creation, dozens, hundreds, thousands, billions and trillions of molecules began bursting out of me, piling on top of one another – immeasurable clouds of early matter spanning many light-years across the empty darkness.

I began creating molecules of different atomic arrangements, mixing and matching them as I spun them around the slowly expanding Universe.

The more I created, the more I understood what I was and what I could become. I understood that if the Universe was an empty stage, I was both the playwright and the play itself. The page was blank and I had only just begun to put pen to paper.

It may be worth noting here that although it is easy enough for me to summarize these cosmic events into briefly worded descriptions, when I actually experienced these things – as sped up as they must have been compared to the *billions* of years that I was apparently witnessing – the visions seemed to go on for an impossibly long time. Granted, time itself became a bit relative, but if I had to guess, I'd estimate that it took at least several decades, perhaps half of the entire 150+ years of the hallucination, to see everything I am now describing in a mere handful of pages. This doesn't particularly matter except to explain where all that time went, for those of you keeping track.

For this reason, I won't harp on it in future sections, but this would not be the last time-guzzling leg of my journey...

Anyway, back to outer space.

I was not content with the stagnation of the elements I had designed. It all felt like a bland, motionless painting. So I created opposing forces of energy – light, gravity, magnetism, and many forces that I could not identify in hindsight – all to push and pull on the molecules so that they would come to life through movement.

I then realized that these molecules had the potential for primitive self-evolving when exposed to the new forces of energy I had created. All they needed in order to progress on their own was time. So I created time.

Now the massive molecular clouds were free to follow their own paths, combining with one another, separating, expanding, contracting, creating new molecules, etc. Eventually the clouds became so enormous that they folded in on themselves, forming dense clusters of gas that erupted in energy and light.

Whole galaxies began lighting up the night sky all around me.

My thoughts fired rapidly, like skipping-stones pitched across a sea of time. I manifest metals and rocks, planets and moons. Every color and texture and temperature and brightness and density imaginable came to life in the growing Cosmos. With every new celestial body I understood more and more about myself.

The Universe of swirling matter was my consciousness transmuted into physical form. Yet, when I spoke to the stars and the planets and the rocks I had created, I saw that they could not answer me. I knew then that Creation was not complete. So I set out to create sentience.

It began with a single cell, just as I had begun as a single molecule. Each cell had miniature functioning parts that allowed for the basic building blocks of movement, growth and self-replication. I whispered to the cells and gave them a primitive awareness that set them above the rocks and planets and stars.

These cells were the seeds of all living Creation. In time, I created a spectacular array of creatures, each with their own unique place in the order of things.

In the blink of an eye, there were mountains and oceans and rivers and forests teeming with life – plants and animals – creatures of all shapes and sizes, all designs imaginable. Each creature perceived its place in the Universe differently from the others, and in doing so taught me something new about myself. Their progress – their evolution – culminated in the design of the Divine Species, mankind, the crown jewel of Creation.

Here, the vision abruptly ended. The creatures and mountains and planets and molecules dissolved like shadows into the black walls of my subconscious.

It was the strangest sensation, a mixture of awe and might. I felt huge and God-like, with the power of Creation at my command, yet miniscule and insignificant in the immense scheme of the Universe.

It was breathtaking and disorienting.

As I sat there in silence for some time, the age-old conundrum dawned on me again. Regardless of whether or not I accepted the fact that God created the observable Universe, if God were once a tiny, lifeless particle floating in empty space, where did this "God particle" come from?

"There was no matter or consciousness before me," God said, "there was only the Spirit."

The Spirit? What does *that* mean??

Well, the word "spirit" is a misnomer because it is so broadly defined, but it's the closest word in the English language that I can attribute it to. It referred to an abstract noun (like "the spirit of Christmas") rather than a concrete noun (like "the spirit of my dead relative"). It's worth remembering that God was not speaking to me in English, per se, but in a supernatural language that I somehow fully understood. The words He used here are a good example of the inherent conflict between that language and my efforts to translate it.

To attempt a complete definition, I'd say that the word "Spirit" in this context refers to a kind of primordial zeitgeist of the Universe – an abstract, non-conscious essence of life that saturates everything, across all dimensions and all planes of existence, on a sub-subatomic level. (In layman nerd-terms, it's sort of like "the Force" in Star Wars. I mean, come on, why overcomplicate it? You're welcome.)

However, its impact on the Universe we see today is so infinitely subtle, that in a very primitive sense, you could argue that the Spirit is the fabric of "nothingness" itself. Therefore, the question of where it came from is a catch-22, like asking where "nothingness" came from.

God explained that this "Spirit" (the essence of life) effectively called the two particles into existence by the crushing weight of its own nothingness and desire for being.

How can "nothingness" call particles into existence? The closest analogy I can give would be the tiny bubbles that appear when you boil water. There appears to be nothing in the water, but as the heat increases, bubbles begin to form in the bottom of the pot. Of course, this is merely the liquid form of water turning into vapor near the heat source, but to the untrained eye, it looks as if something has appeared out of nothing. Likewise, in a *seemingly* empty Universe, the Spirit of Creation lie dormant until the overwhelming burden of its own vast nothingness became so great that tiny particles simply "bubbled" out of it. The particles themselves were the transmutation of the Spirit into a primitive physical form (just like liquid water transforms into water vapor).

When two of these rare, mysterious Spirit-particles collided, consciousness came into existence. That consciousness was what we might call "God" today, that thing which created the observable Universe. In this way, God is miniscule and nothing, just as much as He is massive and

everything.

To recap (because this is some seriously heady shit): God told me that the particle I saw in the beginning of time was simply the byproduct of an empty Universe desperately crying out for sentience. The devastating vacuum of a raw, naked macrocosm became so overwrought with its own lifelessness, that the Universe literally *insisted* upon itself, and thus, God was manifest into awareness, and all of Creation was born through Him.

Whew.

Lastly, God told me that this distinction between "God" (the conscious Deity, the Creator) and "the Spirit" (the non-conscious, spiritual essence of God/the Universe) was the same distinction that the ancient Biblical writers were trying to express through "God the Father" and "the Holy Ghost" – two intrinsically linked but decidedly separate entities.

Put that in your pipe and smoke it…or at least put it in your nitrous oxide mask and nose-pump it.

PART IV: THE TREE OF KNOWLEDGE

All of this led me to the issue of mankind's earliest days – "The Garden of Eden."

I wanted to know how we humans interacted with God in the beginning. And what, if anything, changed from the earliest days to now?

God pulled no punches. He laid it all out with more bizarre detail than I was expecting.

He told me that it was important to understand that in the very beginning, God was ostensibly a kind of outside observer. He was the omnipotent, omnipresent Creator. All the countless billions of galaxies swirling into the far reaches of the Cosmos kept Him thoroughly occupied for what a human mind might consider an eternity. He created all of this in order to better understand Himself and His potential, as well as to satisfy His desire to create. In my hallucination, He called all of this His "macro-creation."

When His mastery of matter and time was complete, His attention turned away from the physical matters of the Universe and instead turned inward, toward the matter of consciousness, that thing which made Him unique and alone in the Universe.

It was then that He decided to create what He called His "micro-creation," planet Earth, a unique world of countless living creatures leading to the evolution of the ultimate species, one that could share in God's knowledge and wonderment – the "Divine Species," as He called it, which would be made in His own image.

Into mankind, God poured true consciousness – an unquenchable thirst for self-awareness, identical to His own. In this way, God told me, humans were "made perfect."

In the early days, Man was isolated in a special realm (perhaps on the planet's surface, although that was not explicitly clear in my vision), a realm that was most certainly outside the normal laws of time and physics as we know them today.

In that place, humans did not eat or sleep, nor did they age. They existed in a physical form, but because they were outside of time, they were untouched by the afflictions of the physical world. Sounds like perfection, right? Well, read on.

I was eager to hear the tale of what happened to that prehistoric paradise, and how we ended up with the non-paradise that included things like genocide, starvation, disease and dental offices...but God became silent, as if He were lost in thought.

Up until this moment, God had been recalling all of this information with a certain sense of giddiness, like an old man being asked about his youth. But now, that joy seemed to fade and His spirits dampened. He just sat there, staring at the dark walls of my subconscious.

He was remembering something from His past, and in the strangest way, I began to sense it, too...

Without warning, I was suddenly overcome by childhood memories.

These were the bittersweet remembrances of places I used to play as a child, alone or with my siblings or cousins. Places that had fallen into neglect or ruin, or worse, had been gutted and replaced by newer, colder edifices.

One memory in particular stood above the rest. It was of an old tree on my family's property in Virginia with branches full of thorns that bore large, inedible fruit. We used to play on those branches. We called it the Thorn Tree.

It was near the creek, a couple hundred yards from the back porch of the house, on the edge of a field where we kept a handful of sheep. There was an enormous turn-of-the-century barn that was covered in thick vines overlooking the Thorn Tree. We didn't play in the barn, partly because it was on the neighbor's property, but mostly because it was dark and scary and full of snakes.

I remembered my cousin Timmy and I building dams in the creek to make small wading pools. We built wood forts and stone paths, then sat high in the Thorn Tree to reign over our make-believe kingdom.

Timmy once refused to walk back to the house with me to go to the bathroom. Instead, he taught me how to dig a hole and shit in it like a man.

Today, the creek is all but dried up, just a trickle of water, lined with old tires and Styrofoam cups. The forts and stone paths were all washed away in floodwaters. Our little kingdom, the Thorn Tree and all, is now buried under mud, trash and thick brush.

The old barn was torn down ten or fifteen years ago to be sold as salvage wood. The sheep all died in a lightening storm, and weeds overtook the field.

Cousin Timmy lost most of his hair, and goes by "Tim" now. I'm lucky if I see him once every year or so. We get along great for old times' sake, though our political views are starkly opposed and we certainly aren't close enough to shit in the woods together anymore.

Perhaps worse than any of these things is the question of whether or not children even play like that anymore, in imagination and nature, away from all the gadgets and websites.

Anyway, it may have (literally) been a shit hole, but it was my youth. It was a country lad's paradise, in its own way. And it was all gone.

Why was I suddenly remembering all this?

God hadn't said a word, but I somehow knew what He was thinking in His melancholy silence. I could feel it.

The "Garden of Eden" was gone forever, and God missed it. It was the same kind of feeling that I imagine a parent feels looking back on a child's playroom long after the child is grown. Somehow, my subconscious was all that was left of that timeless paradise that God had designed for early humanity. We were standing in the sad, desolate remains of the Garden of Eden, stripped of all its life and color – the trees and fruits and creature companions – all of it had been reduced to this tiny shard of near nothingness. A dark void, hidden in the deepest of earthly caverns: the human mind.

To be clear, when Eden was abandoned by God and Men (a story we will get to shortly), it ceased to exist in a physical form. Instead, it became nothing but a tiny mark on the souls of all mankind, a subconscious reminder of our youth and innocence as a species – before we were touched by death and war and greed and sickness. This "mark of Eden" is hidden away deep in our spirits, only a miniscule fragment of the original place in which God and humanity once dwelled together. A sliver that every man and woman possesses somewhere in their minds.

By arriving in this place, with God, it felt like I had accidentally discovered a hidden chamber in one of the Egyptian pyramids – a place that was secretly just behind the ancient walls that had been so thoroughly explored by others.

God just looked at me, knowingly. I didn't say anything. There was nothing to say. I just nodded, signaling to Him that I empathized with His sadness. In a way, I too longed for Eden again.

It was strange…sensing God's sadness. It's one emotion we don't usually associate with the Almighty, but there it was. It wasn't some kind of massive, God-like heaviness, but a small, simple, almost human sort of emotional weight. In light of everything I had seen thus far – the beacons of light in the outer reaches of space, the formation of the stars and planets, the evolution of Man – this small, gentle *emotion* coming from the Creator felt the most profound.

Finally, He broke the silence. "This is all that remains," He said.

"Of the Garden of Eden?" I asked.

He smiled, humorlessly, and said, "Of my youth. And of humanity's infancy."

Then God sat up and seemed to shake Himself out of it. "That time was destined to pass away," He said, "and this time was destined to come."

Then, He began to explain the details of what happened in Eden.

He told me how He shared His knowledge with mankind there in that prehistoric realm (a place called "Eden" in the Judeo-Christian tradition, though God never called it that in my vision). Humans saw that they were made in the image of God, but knew they were not gods themselves. They understood that they were the bearers of consciousness, the Divine Species, set above all else. And once they understood these things thoroughly, they longed not only to know what it meant to be aware, like God was, but also what it meant to be unaware, like the other animals. They wanted to know both parts of themselves: the part that was made like god (the mind) and the part that was made like animal (the body).

In short, they longed to know what it was to be human.

This thirst for self-knowledge would prove to be humanity's blessing and its curse, inherited directly from their Creator.

There in the Garden (or whatever you're most comfortable calling it), mankind watched as the animals of the Earth drew breath, ate, slept, reproduced, grew old and died. They desired to know all of these things for themselves, but they could not because they were not part of the natural cycle of the Earth. They were separated, protected, from those things.

In this way, "the Garden" was only a temporary cage for early humans, a cage designed to be broken when mankind was ready.

God confessed that He had given them the minds and the desires to explore the vast world He had created, yet upon seeing them, He grew reluctant to let them go. He knew He couldn't ask them to stay, because it would prohibit them from the richness of their journey in the Universe. It would have been like asking a starving man to sit at your banquet table but not allowing him to eat.

After an untold numbers of days, years or possibly eons (time was irrelevant to them, so I can't tell how long they existed in this way), the early humans asked to leave the protection of the Garden.

Despite the fact that God knew humans would have this desire (and moreover, He *designed* them to have this desire), He allowed us to choose our own fate. And so we did. In short, we chose existential knowledge over the safety of immortality.

This was, of course, another paradox. God knew how it would all turn out, yet let us choose our own path: a predestined free will. I was starting to get use to these kinds of mind-benders.

But why would we leave paradise to suffer like animals?

Well, according to God, given the choice between an eternal life of limited comprehension of emotion, sentience and truth, we, as a collective species, chose to reach for the extremes and experience everything that life had to offer.

It'd be like asking a professional mountain climber why they wanted to climb Mt. Kilimanjaro. It's too difficult, and it's dangerous! Other people have already climbed it. Just watch a documentary or look at pictures. The mountain climber may not be able to tell you exactly why she needs to experience it for herself, it's just part of her nature. We were *designed* to crave existential knowledge, just as God Himself does.

Now here's where the story gets interesting.

It was understood by all parties involved that once mankind was released into the world, they would have to survive on their own, like all the other animals God had created. Otherwise, Man would simply always call on God to fix things, and naturally, God would always do it because He cared about our well-being. Neither mankind nor God would be able to authentically experience the Universe unless they both agreed to sever their link and go their separate ways.

Because these early humans were involved in establishing the first settlements on Earth, God referred to them as "the Council" or "the Founders." This "Council" also helped establish the guidelines for how and when God would interact with humans on Earth. Together they made a sort of pact. God vowed never to force His will upon humans, or divert their destinies for any reason. He knew this would inevitably leave humans in a world full of distress, confusion and superstition, but all of these things were part of what both God and mankind were longing to understand.

It seems strange from our perspective today to think that when God first created humans, they didn't understand things like fear, loss, confusion, hunger, etc. Likewise, they were incapable of fully comprehending happiness, love, fulfillment, etc., because none of these things *can* be understood without the other.

Boiled down to Judeo-Christian terms, they sought "the knowledge of good and evil." It wasn't that they desired to know "evil," necessarily, but they knew that "good" could not exist without it. Like Yin and Yang, they are two halves of a whole. Today, we tend to look at such things as if they are separate forces, but in my hallucination, they were not. They were (and are) a single, inseparable unit.

Therefore, the same force that drives us to love and laugh and forgive and connect with others also drives us to hate and weep and curse and detach. You cannot attain one set of these conditions without also accepting the other. In the deepest parts of ourselves (both us and God), there is even a thirst for suffering, just as strong as our thirst for happiness, though it is often rejected by our conscious minds.

God and the early humans understood all this, and the legacy of that wisdom lives on in various philosophies and faith traditions today.

All of these things – the Council, the protected realm, the necessity of good and evil, etc. – were crudely translated by the descendants of the early humans into what ultimately became the book of Genesis and other religious histories. The story was simplified into basic allegorical components: a man and a woman choosing to eat from "the Tree of Knowledge" over God's offering of "the Tree of Life" and they were therefore separated from God.

It seems reasonable to assume that my subconscious mind was at work here, rewriting old ideas into a form that I was more willing to accept than the Bible stories I learned as a kid. That reasoning makes sense up to a point, but the "Garden" was only the first half of this creation story.

The second half got a lot weirder.

PART V: THE FIRST AGE

Like *Alice in Wonderland*, the story only got stranger the deeper I slipped into it. This is where my creationist journey began to cross out of Genesis and into uncharted waters.

God told me that mankind's one reluctance to leave their isolation in "the Garden" was that they knew the link between them and God would be cut. This was the first fear born in the minds of Men, the fear of separation from God.

Because of this fear, God and the Council of Men made a pact in which God agreed to stay with the early humans for about 1000 years to help prepare them for their independence. After that, God was to remain in partial communication with them for *another* 1000 years, essentially to wean them off of His guidance and oversight. God referred to this two thousand year time period as "the First Age."

I know, I know…this is some seriously crazy shit. I have no idea what kind of drugs instigate these kinds of hyper-detailed stories on behalf of their users, but this is what I was told in my hallucination – a straight-up mythological pre-history of early humanity. Enjoy.

In order to give early humans a leg up on survival, God gave the Founders a few special traits that distinguished them from any of their descendants (including us modern humans). First, they had direct access to God. They called, He answered. It was as simple as that. Second, they had extraordinarily long lives. Literally, some lived for hundreds of years, outliving multiple generations of their own children.

Because of these two things, the Founders were revered for many generations as sages, elders and even demigods. As the time passed and they eventually all died off, their stories were handed down through oral tradition and slipped into legend. These legends formed the basis of almost every heroic, supernatural act in all of the world's ancient religious texts/oral traditions. I'm talkin' the Greeks, the Romans, the Egyptians, the Mayans, the Babylonians – all of them.

God never said explicitly how many Founders there were during this time, but there were clearly enough to divide them into groups and scatter them across the Earth in such a way as to breed maximum diversity (according to God's plan). If I were to guess, I'd say that their numbers must have been in the hundreds, if not thousands. Each group was able to develop their own culture and find their own unique path towards civilization.

But let's back up for a bit.

During the first 1000 years, God lived amongst the Founders and counseled them as planned. He mediated mankind's early conflicts and influenced civil guidelines for the emerging civilizations. He gave them knowledge over the plants that grew near each colony, so that they could feed themselves and heal their ailments. God communicated directly with the Founders whenever they asked for Him in prayer.

Today, "prayer" is more like a meditation than a real conversation. You pray quietly to yourself and no one answers – or, at least, no one literally speaks back to you. This was not the case back then, apparently. During these early days, God manifested Himself on the Earth in physical form. He would appear to the Founders as pure light, as plants, as beasts, as the elements of water, rock and fire, as apparitions and other mystical visages.

As time passed, and the first 1000 years expired, God began communicating less and less directly. He began appearing only in dreams and visions to guide people. This kind of guidance encouraged mankind to look not only to God for help, but also to look within themselves, thusly preparing them for self-sufficiency. The dreams and visions from God *required* human interpretation, which allowed mankind's own inner spirit to begin leading the way.

This was the dawn of "spirituality" as we know it today.

By the end of the Age, God ceased all communication between Himself and the early humans. Even the dreams and visions stopped, marking the first true separation between Man and God.

Through this separation, mankind came to truly know *fear* for the first time – a fear so great, that it still dwells within us all today, at the very foundation of our spirits – the fear of being alone in the Universe, without God. And somehow, through this immense fear, *love* became illuminated for the first time as well.

Love and fear collided, in this moment, instantly defining one another like shadow and light. According to God, something in the very fabric of the Cosmos shifted that day. He called it "the awakening of the Universe."

This "awakening" was essentially the birth of *emotion* for both God and Man: love and fear being our prime emotions – the mother and father of our emotional senses, if you will – from which all other emotions stem.

And with that, humankind was left on Earth alone (as we are today), and God was sequestered to the abstract heavens (as He seems to be today).

Once again, there is some difficulty in translating God's words into English here. The word "fear," in this context, was used to describe a love-based fear, if that makes any sense. It's like the fear of losing someone you love, for example, rather than a general fear of something "bad." It's an important distinction.

The fear described above is like the shadow of love itself.

Imagine, if you will, "love" as a pure white box against a pure white background. Without shadow, the box is indistinguishable from the background and you can't see it at all. Only with its shadow is the box revealed. That's the relationship of love and fear that I saw in God's words.

As He told me all of these things about mankind's early days on Earth, I had another memory from my own childhood flash across the forefront of my mind.

It was of my father teaching me how to ride a bike.

This memory is almost embarrassing to recount because of how cliché it sounds. It's Americana kitsch lifted straight out of *The Andy Griffith Show* or *Leave It To Beaver*.

My dad had taken the training wheels off the bike, and I sat atop it, petrified of falling over. The goal was to ride to the top of our long driveway and back with Dad running alongside me, holding the seat and keeping the bike upright as I pedaled and steered.

At the base of the driveway, just as the wheels started to move, I nervously called out to him, "Don't go too fast."

He said, "Okay, I won't push at all. Go at whatever speed you want, and tell me when you want me to let go."

I pedaled slowly all the way to the top of the driveway, careful not to go any faster than my dad could run.

I slowly turned the bike around, built up my courage and said, "Okay, Dad...let go, and I'll ride back to the house by myself."

After a moment, I heard my father's voice somewhere in the distance shouting, "What??"

I hit the brakes and looked up to see that he had never left the base of the driveway. I had done it all by myself. He just smiled and waved proudly.

I took off riding all over the yard, having been lured into confidence.

So, I suppose you could say that for humanity, the First Age was the "training wheel phase" of the ride yet to come.

As time passed and the last remaining Founders finally grew old and perished, God told me it became increasingly unbearable for Him to stand idly by as humans began to forget who He truly was, and instead began crafting new versions of "God" that represented whatever they *wanted* Him to be.

Through mythology, lore and outright manipulation, humans took the stories of God and the Founders and turned them into conflicting superstitions, which in turn fueled bloodshed on Earth. Within only a few generations, God's legacy was reduced to an inventive assortment of gods and demons, idols and rules.

Humanity was no longer guided by a quest for truth, as God and the Council had anticipated, but by various alternative desires, like worldly comforts, order, power and greed. To accomplish this, people began using superstitions (the early prototypes of what eventually became full-fledged religions) to manipulate others and bring order to the emerging civilizations. The leaders of these early societies, who often called themselves gods (or representatives of gods), could easily convince their superstitious subjects to do nearly anything – obey rules, hand over food and coin, go to war, sacrifice their own children, anything.

This use of religion to gain power and to exploit the powerless has, sadly, never been fully resolved since those early days. It has only become more discreet, and more cunning, in its manipulation tactics.

Luckily for us, all was not lost. God devised a plan that would counteract the effects of manmade religious superstitions, and guide humanity back towards Him.

He returned to the timeless realm, the abandoned "Garden" that He had shown me earlier, and reassembled the souls of all the original Founders.

For fun, let's call this the "Ghost Council" (God never called them that, but that's kind of what they were). Imagine every god and demigod and hero ever mentioned in the all the various mythologies of the ancient world, all assembled in one place! This was a meeting of truly epic proportion.

Unlike before, the "Council" now had earthly life experience under their collective belts. These experiences allowed them to explain to God what, if anything, He could do to better understand humanity's desires on Earth, and thusly, help God protect humans from harming one another (or themselves) in light of their separation from Him.

Since this all occurred outside the traditional sense of time, the meeting went on for an untold number of years, during which the "Ghost Council" agreed upon two world-altering amendments to the original contract between God and human beings.

The first was in regards to God's communication with Man. While direct communication was still considered too aggressive, the Council accepted the use of dreams and visions as a means for God's voice to permeate the earthly realm. As long as the will of God was only suggested, not imposed, the communication was permissible. This allowed God to influence humans indirectly, but it also became less likely for humans to believe that God had abandoned them, or that He had never existed at all. Dreams and visions left just enough room for the thin thread of faith to remain intact. And so it was done.

The second major amendment was in regards to God's place within Creation itself. The Ghost Council's testimony convinced God that if He wished to *truly* understand the experiences of humans on Earth, to know Creation from the inside out, it wasn't enough for Him to be an outside observer. God would have to taste the proverbial 'fruit' for Himself and walk the Earth, not as a god, but as a mortal.

God would have to become *human*.

PART VI: JESUS CHRIST SUPERNOVA

Most Christians believe in a God consisting of three separate parts, a complicated doctrine they call "the Trinity": God the Father, God the Son and the Holy Ghost. While this trifecta was not precisely the way God described Himself to me, I quickly discovered why there was some confusion as He and I continued to discuss the intricacies of His existence.

I had thus far accounted for two of the three "God-parts" during my hallucination. The identity of "God the Father" was pretty straightforward. He was the *Entity* with which I was communicating. The "Holy Ghost" was portrayed to me as the "God-essence" that permeates all things (as discussed in Part III of this chapter). That left only one theological stone unturned – "God the Son."

I wasn't about to have a 200-year conversation with God without getting some answers about the man who almost single-handedly shaped Western civilization.

Well, buckle up. No matter if you're a raging Atheist or a Bible-thumping Christian, I guarantee you're going to hate what He had to tell me. Consider this fair warning.

"The man you call Jesus Christ was me, in human form," God said plainly.

Ugh.

My father was going to rub this in my face for the rest of my life. I met God on an accidental drug trip and He told me that Jesus was real.

Gross.

All of the Atheists and other non-Christians probably just stopped reading my book. Thanks, Jesus.

"However," He continued, "most of what you know about Jesus Christ, most of what has been written about him, is untrue."

Oh, boy.

Now all of the Christians probably just stopped reading my book. Thanks, Jesus!

Okay, if there's anyone out there left reading at this point, you're probably some moderate-hippy-sicko, in which case *you* might actually get a kick out of the next couple heretical subchapters.

Regardless, for the remainder of this section I'll focus on the concept of God becoming human and, more specifically, why this event was important.

In the section that follows, Part VII, I'll get into the specifics of what God told me about Jesus's actual life and death—a story I like to call, "The Gospel According to Nitrous Oxide." If you didn't grow up with Christianity or just don't have any interest in the life of Christ, you have my full permission to skip it. However, to understand the overall message of this book, you should at least get through the remainder of this subchapter. (It's like less than five pages. You'll make it.)

First, God explained precisely what it meant for Him to become human, and why He did it.

He told me that Christ was merely the human vessel into which God poured Himself in order to understand the world from the inside. To do this, He had to strip Himself of His God-consciousness. That is, while He was in human form, He had no idea that He had ever been anything other than just a man.

God suspended His knowledge and dominion over all things, and saw the world just as mankind does. He had no memory of having ever been "God." He did not know that the entire Universe had been created by His own hands. He did not know whether or not His life had any meaning or purpose, nor how it might end. When He looked up into the sky and prayed as a man, He did not know that He was praying to Himself.

For the record, God was explicitly telling me that Jesus Christ did not know (or even remotely believe) that he *was* God incarnate. This is of particular interest because it's the opposite of what most Christians believe today.

God continued, explaining that walking the earth in human form was not merely a divine experiment. It was much more important than that. Through Christ's death God intended to transform Himself, forever.

By entering the world in human form, God's goal was not only to gain the existential knowledge of what it meant to be human, but also to transform Himself *through that knowledge* so that He would never be separated from us again. To do this, God knew He had to stop being an outside observer, but instead, He had to merge Himself, permanently, into His Creation.

This is obviously a tricky concept, so let me use an analogy.

Imagine God, the outside observer, as a tiny green worm who is aware of the possibility of becoming a butterfly. In this scenario, Jesus was merely the thin *cocoon* into which God dwelled, temporarily, in order to achieve His goal. The new-God, the "butterfly," that emerged after the death of Christ was far more profound than Christ himself.

Ironically, in the aftermath of Jesus's death, almost everyone seemed to fixate on the cocoon rather than the butterfly that emerged from it, but that's a whole other story, I suppose.

God told me that upon His death as a human (Christ's death), He literally became joined together with *every living thing* on Earth, including every single human being, and ceased being the outside observer, aloof in the heavens.

How can this be? How could God become merged with every living thing, all at once?

He explained this phenomenon to me through a vision, telling me that Christ's death was a kind of spiritual "supernova" for God himself.

In order to understand this vision, you first need to understand what a supernova is. In case you are not keen on astrophysics, a supernova is a massive star that explodes at the end of its lifecycle.

Normally, the churning energy within a star's core pushes outward into space (radiating light and fiery gases), while the gravitational force of the star is constantly pushing against it, inward. These two forces, pushing against each other, keep the star smoldering in space until the energy in the core weakens over time (billions of years) and can no longer hold off gravity. When this happens, gravity wins the pushing match and crushes the giant star, which condenses all of the remaining energy into a tiny volatile ball. This eventually triggers a massive explosion, sending stardust and energy blazing in all directions. This is a supernova explosion.

Through this act, the giant star effectively dies, but its particles and energy spread across the galaxy, merging with other interstellar mediums and beginning a whole new life cycle for all the starstuff around it.

The etymology of the word comes from the Latin "super" (meaning "beyond") and "nova" (meaning "new"). By this definition, a supernova explosion literally makes the star "beyond new" – which is precisely why I think God chose this analogy to explain His transfiguration to me.

He asked me to imagine a giant star, blazing for eons in the suspended heavens. As soon as I began to focus on it, I felt a rush of wind and a stomach-sinking sensation…

Swoosh!

Once again I was whisked away into the Cosmos.

I saw a massive star, burning in bright red-orange colors. The star gently pulsed as its heat radiated over my body. I could sense how ancient the star was, billions of years old. It was coming to the end of its life as a colossal giant in the sky, and was about to begin a new journey.

The star swelled outward in all directions, taking one deep, final breath before the end. Then, in hyper speed, it began to shrink, caving in on itself, transforming before my eyes.

Its color changed from dark red to orange, then yellow, blue and indigo as it got smaller and smaller, until finally, it was only a tiny ball of pure white light.

This white blot in space was the same star as before, only it had been transformed from its monolithic state into this tiny speck. The star existed like this for some time, but its condensed form was only temporary (it was its "cocoon" state), a gateway towards an even greater metamorphosis.

Time swept by at a frenzied pace, until the tiny white star became silent and brighter than ever.

"Shield your eyes," God whispered.

The small white star exploded in a thunderous blast of color, heat and light. I could feel its shattered particles pelting across my face like sharp, horizontal rain, or sand ripping across a stormy beach.

I intellectually knew that this was all some kind of grand hallucination, yet I instinctively raised my hands over my face and turned away from the surge of flame and stardust blowing past.

"This is the supernova," God shouted over the chaos, "the natural life cycle of the star."

Then, in a flash, it was over, and the vacuum of ether around us began to feel quiet and cool.

I slowly opened my eyes and gasped as I peered out into the galaxy.

An endless mist of stardust, glimmering as far as the eye could see, replaced what had been empty black space before – every color imaginable, gently swirling and dancing translucently through the Cosmos, just waiting to spring to new life.

God explained that the matter and energy of the star was still the same, only burst apart now into countless tiny fragments that would soon spread across the Universe, beginning yet another journey. (In other words, the energy of the star had not changed, but its *function* in the Universe had.)

Through this natural cycle of celestial things, God was showing me the pattern He followed in His own metamorphic journey.

To be clear, God was suggesting that He had condensed Himself down into a single human being (Jesus), and that upon His death on Earth, His soul burst apart into countless fragments so that those innumerable pieces of Him could be planted into *each and every living thing* in the Universe, thereby joining God (literally) with His Creation, until the end of time.

In this way, God made it so that He could never be separated from mankind again.

This would perhaps become the most defining revelation in my entire encounter. God Himself had burst apart into countless tiny God-particles, and each of those particles settled deep inside all living things, deep inside every man and woman on Earth...including one such particle inside of *me*.

It was that tiny piece of God, dwelling inside me, that I was communicating with.

This realization that God was a part of me, just as I was a part of Him, gave me an overwhelming sense of comfort, of togetherness, of *completeness*, that until this moment I had never known.

Christ, then, was a sort of template. He was the first human being to hold God within himself. Now, every human being holds God within him or herself. In this way, we are all "Christians," at least in the technical sense of the word. We are all "Christ-like," because we all have God dwelling within us, just has Christ did.

This is the meaning of the Biblical phrase, "Emmanuel" (which means "God with us"). The phrase is used by Christians today to refer to Christ, but in my hallucination, God said it actually referred to all of us, because God is literally *with us* now.

According to God, whether you've heard or care about the stories of Christ's life or not is irrelevant. And, whether you realize or care that

God is within you or not is irrelevant. It's all true, nonetheless.

"Because of this, I am with you always," God said, "and so the Divine Species is finally complete."

Years after my trip, my wife and I were talking about this particular part of my hallucination.

She couldn't get her mind around the notion that God could create something (humans, namely) without fully understanding exactly what He had created. So much so, He had to enter the world as a human Himself, just to understand His own design. To her, it was like suggesting that a clockmaker could build a functioning timepiece without understanding how it actually worked. It didn't make sense.

A clockmaker is a bad example, though, because he cannot possibly live within or become a part of his clock. A better example would be something like a playwright.

Suppose a playwright constructs a new play, then gets into rehearsals and realizes that the actors are having a different experience working on the piece than he had expected. So much so that, eventually, in order to truly understand the characters he'd written, the playwright would have to enter the stage and play a role himself.

This analogy is better because it implies a *living* creation that grows and evolves, as opposed to a hard creation that is stationary and lifeless. My wife (at the time) found this comparison helpful, so I thought I'd share it with you.

Interestingly, perhaps because she was raised as an indifferent sort of Catholic (who later became decidedly Agnostic), she had no problem with my hallucinogenic thesis on God's supernova-like transformation through Christ. Her attitude was somewhere in the vein of: "Well yeah, that makes sense."

She is, therefore, the first honorary disciple of the Gospel According to Nitrous Oxide.

PART VII:
THE GOSPEL ACCORDING TO NITROUS OXIDE
(ABRIDGED)

The life of Jesus Christ has fueled one of the world's largest religions for 2000 years, divided amongst thousands of denominations, as well as several spin-off religions and a plethora of fan fiction in the form of books (like this one!), plays, movies and an entire genre of really terrible music.

Again, if you're one of those people who gets uncomfortable with Jesus-talk, feel free to skip ahead to the next section. No offense taken. Likewise, if you're one of those people who just can't talk about Jesus enough, you might also want to skip ahead, because this section is just bound to upset you. Fair warning.

I offer it only for those curious as to what I heard and saw in my hallucination regarding the life and times of Jesus. Take it or leave it.

I can't tell how much time we spent reviewing Christ's life, but it felt like a large percentage of my hallucination, in retrospect. It was almost as if I were witnessing his entire life in real-time, as some kind of ghost. And that's what I wanted. I wanted Christ's entire story, from Christmas to Easter.

Was he born from a virgin? Did he heal the sick and walk on water? Did he rise from the dead? What *really* happened?!

I'm happy to report that God answered all of these questions and more. The account was remarkably detailed, and more than I could possibly have hoped for.

The Gospel story I witnessed in my hallucination was like a super-heretical Sunday School class, and I was okay with that. I was relieved that my whole trip wasn't descending into pure pro-Bible propaganda. While there was a lot of familiar territory within the story, there were also a lot of bizarre, left-field tidbits about Jesus's life that I was completely unprepared for.

Interestingly, my Christian friends often hear these parts of the Jesus story and ask things like, "Where did you come up with all that?" or "Are there any dead sea scrolls or Bible verses that can confirm any of this?" Without a doubt, the answer is: absolutely not. It's important that this point is made clear.

In no uncertain terms, half the things God told me about Jesus's life do not correlate with any ancient writings about Jesus that I'm aware of. Again, the purpose of this section is merely to tell you what I was told. I am not attempting to "prove" that these events actually happened; there is no way of doing so, even if I wanted to. I'm just the messenger.

Let me start at the beginning.

Brace yourself, this first part is a little intense. And there is no way for me to sugarcoat it.

God told me that He did not mysteriously impregnate a virgin in order to conceive Christ. The truth was that Jesus's mother, Mary, had been raped at the age of 12 or 13 by a local boy, and in order for her not to be shamed (or even condemned to death, which was not uncommon for a rape victim at the time), a local widower named Joseph was convinced by the town's rabbi to wed Mary, thereby providing her protection. Joseph was reluctant, and ended up being ridiculed by the townspeople for marrying so young a girl after the recent death of his first wife. The scandal only worsened when word spread that Mary was pregnant. Joseph had been working as a carpenter, but rumors and slander rendered him virtually unemployable. This quickly prompted the couple to leave town altogether, in search of a new home, despite the fact that poor Mary was with child.

This desperate search for work led Joseph and Mary to the town of Bethlehem, where Mary went into labor. Penniless, they begged a local innkeeper for shelter until Mary had given birth. The innkeeper refused to give them a proper room without being paid, but reluctantly allowed them to stay in the shed behind the inn, with the other travelers' animals, on account of the fact that she was in labor.

The version of the story that's written in the Bible was, according to the God in my head, altered by the early Church in order to increase its dramatic/mystical value. Mary was impregnated by immaculate conception, there was a "census" that brought Joseph and Mary to Bethlehem, and there was simply no room at the inn, which forced the warmhearted innkeeper to open his stables for them. Not so far off, but not quite the truth.

Joseph eventually found work in a town called Nazareth. He and Mary started a new life there, free of scandal and shame. Nonetheless, Joseph grew cold towards the young Jesus, because he secretly blamed the boy for all of these trials.

Joseph was an incredibly devout man (which is why he agreed to wed poor Mary in the first place, by order of the rabbi). So when Jesus was only a child, he began to study the scriptures intently because he thought it would please his father. It worked, and the two bonded over the scrolls.

As Jesus grew older, he got mixed up with a group of Jewish rebels who wanted to raise an army to overthrow the Romans who occupied their territories – these rebels were called the "Zealots." Although Jesus ultimately disassociated with them because he disagreed with their violent intentions, his connection with the Zealots led to his downfall. However, it was also through these rebels that Jesus met several of his earliest and most loyal disciples (including "Simon the Zealot").

Joseph despised the Zealots because he believed they would spur the wrath of the Romans against the Jews (which they ultimately did). When Jesus became involved with them, Joseph all but disowned him in protest. Jesus and his father never made amends before Joseph died unexpectedly, a fact that Jesus regretted all his life.

With his father dead, and the Zealots furious at him for abandoning their cause, Jesus traveled around the lands nearby, meeting many different sects of Jews – including Jewish Mystics – as well as non-Jews from other parts of the world, all of which impacted his future ministry.

For some time, Jesus followed a traveling Jewish preacher called John the Baptist. (In the Bible, John is identified as Jesus's cousin, but in my vision this was not true.) Jesus admired much of John's teaching, though he disagreed with the necessity of water baptisms, which was obviously the cornerstone of John's ministry. John was something of a hippy, so he didn't mind that he and Jesus did not agree on all theological doctrines. The important thing that John did in Jesus's life was create a template for teaching that Jesus was able to adapt.

Eventually, Jesus began his own ministry. Several of John's followers left John's camp in order to follow Jesus instead (including a man who would later become Jesus's closest disciple and friend, "Peter").

Unlike in the Bible, Jesus preached almost exclusively about the transfiguration of the material world into a spiritual world. That is, that "Heaven" was attainable on Earth, just as "Hell" could be manifested on Earth. The idea of Heaven being a reward for good behavior and Hell being a punishment for bad behavior in some kind of afterlife scenario would have been too rudimentary for Christ's highly philosophical teachings.

He preached that God did not want people to follow the old sacred laws merely for the sake of some afterlife reward, but rather, He wanted them to have universal compassion towards one another for the sake of bettering their lives here on Earth. This is why he said things to his disciples like, "Some who are standing here will not taste death before they see the Kingdom of God."[8] He was saying that some of his disciples would find true peace through human kindness before they died, not that the "apocalypse" was coming within the disciples' lifetimes (which, er, it didn't).

Jesus had both male and female disciples – fourteen of them, according to my vision. He had a serious romantic relationship with Mary Magdalene, who was not a prostitute (and sorry *Da Vinci Code* fans, but no, they never had children).

Even more fun than all that, Jesus had a sense of humor. I can't tell you how much better the story gets with Jesus cracking jokes the whole time. Okay, maybe he wasn't a stand-up comic, but he had the ability to make a quip on occasion. For example, the famous phrase from the original Gospels, "The spirit is willing, but the body is weak," wasn't just some serious lecture in the Garden of Gethsemane, it was a catchphrase that cracked Jesus up whenever he or one of his disciples got too tired to continue working (they usually used it in reference to Peter, who could apparently sleep through anything). Another example, when some guy on the street tried to belittle Jesus's preaching by asking if Jesus could "heal him" from chronic masturbation, Jesus told him: "Cut off your right hand, or whatever part of your body causes you to sin." He meant it as a wisecrack, but it somehow got added into the "Sermon on the Mount."[9] Out of context, the statement is just oddly severe.

These kinds of details – the stories about how he met each of the disciples, his relationships he had with this family, how the rumors began spreading that he was a miracle worker, how Judas never really betrayed him, and much more – are all super interesting to me, but not incredibly essential to the message of this book I'm writing. For this reason, I won't continue to burden you with additional details here. (However, if there appears to be any interest in a full account of The Gospel According to

Nitrous Oxide, I am happy to publish it separately sometime in the future.)

Before we leave this section, though, let me mention a few heavy-hitting story points that surround Jesus's death.

It all started when Jesus and his disciples intentionally fulfilled one of the "signs of the Messiah" from the old holy texts (riding a donkey into the city of Jerusalem[10]) in order to draw attention to their cause, which was to change the world by transforming the way in which people perceived it (*perceive* your neighbor as yourself, *perceive* your enemy as your friend, *perceive* Heaven around you instead of Hell, etc.). They wanted the Jews to *perceive* a spiritual king that could overthrow all oppression, instead of waiting for a literal king to show up and simply overthrow the Romans, which is what most Jews were hoping for at the time (including the rebel "Zealots"). By fulfilling the signs of the Messiah, all in the name of peace and spirituality rather than war, Jesus hoped to reform the spirit of Judaism.

The good news was that this tactic did get everyone's attention. The bad news was that it also got Jesus killed.

The Zealots were already mad at Jesus for not helping them raise an army against the Romans, but when he entered Jerusalem on the back of a donkey (symbolically declaring himself the liberating "King of Israel"), the Zealots launched a plan against him. They went straight to their enemy, the Romans, and proclaimed that Jesus was coming to raise a Jewish rebellion against them. That's right; they accused Jesus of being one of *them*! And it worked! The Roman authorities immediately called for his arrest.

The rest, as they say, is history.

Jesus was eventually put to death by the Romans for attempting to lead a rebellion against Caesar. For his messianic stunt on the donkey, they jokingly nailed a sign above his head as he died on the cross which read, "King of the Jews."

Now, this is the part of the story that my Christian friends despise the most, and my non-Christian friends just shrug off.

In my vision, Jesus was not resurrected from the dead (at least, not literally). For many Christians, this is a deal breaker. I can't say that I totally understand why. To me, it always seemed like Jesus's *dying* was the important part of the story (the whole "he died for our sins" thing), and that the resurrection was just icing on the cake that added an impressive supernatural layer to the story.

But then, what do I know?

PART VIII: Money Makes the Church Go Around

In truth, all of these things about Jesus's life and death make perfect sense coming from the brain of a guy in the twenty-first century who grew up studying the Bible. For better or worse, all of my problems with the whole "Jesus thing" were resolved through this hallucination, and that caused an important realization for me. Regardless of how I came to it, there was clearly a part of me that still cherished Christ's teachings. And there was something beautiful about that self-awareness. It gave me permission to be okay with those teachings while abandoning the superstitions of the Church. This was incredibly freeing for me.

Then God dropped a critical piece of the puzzle on me. After what felt like years of storytelling about Jesus, He told me that none of what He had said about Christ's life was important.

Let me repeat that: None of what He had said about Christ's life was important.

It didn't matter if I knew all of these details or not. It didn't matter if *anyone* knew these details or not. God's gift of "salvation" to mankind was completely unconditional (unlike in the Bible, which insists that salvation is only for those who agree with, well, the Bible).

God said it didn't matter if anyone even knew that Jesus existed at all. The act of God living and dying on Earth – the act itself – was all that ever mattered. It was not important whether or not anyone ever *knew* that it happened. Does that distinction make sense?

My mind reeled over this stuff.

Having grown up an evangelical Southern Baptist, I couldn't quite digest the idea that Jesus's life story wasn't somehow crucial for every human being to be made aware of, especially now that I knew all of the answers! But God explained, rather pointedly, that if it had been important that the details of Christ's life be recorded and known to all the world, Jesus himself would have written them down, or, at the very least, ordered his disciples to do so. Considering that Jesus never wrote a book, nor did he explicitly instruct anyone else to write a book (either in my vision or in the original Biblical text), I couldn't really argue with God on this one. Besides, since God *was* Jesus, He had this discussion pretty much locked down.

In the Bible, Jesus did instruct his disciples to spread his teachings "to all the nations of the world" (after he allegedly rose from the dead). That's the closest thing he ever said to "write a bunch of books and build a massive religious institution," so most Christians just use that one passage to broadly explain everything that happened in the centuries following his death. But based on everything else the Bible says about Jesus's mission, the implication of that passage was more likely that they should travel the world and preach in the same way that Jesus had been doing, and the same way that John the Baptist had been doing before him. Considering that all of his disciples were most likely illiterate (scholars believe that less than 10% of the population could read at the time, and even fewer could write[11]), it was highly unlikely that Jesus would have ordered all of his friends to write books. Regardless, there is also a big difference between asking them to continue preaching his sermons versus asking them to document his personal life story. Whatever argument there may be for the former, there certainly is none for the latter.

God told me that it was never important for the "salvation of human souls" that mankind understand who He was in human form. He sacrificed Himself, in order to save humanity from being alone. That sacrifice was an unconditional gift to the human race, because He loved them. Besides, what kind of God would He be if He only rescued a select few of His children from the fires of Hell? When God wants to give humans something, He just gives it to them. There's no price tag, there's no puzzle to solve, no stipulations – God is more powerful than any of that. At least, the God I met was.

The traditional Christian viewpoint suggests that God created some kind of superstitious obstacle course, a spiritual riddle that every man must solve in order to get into Heaven, and those who fail are set on fire for eternity. This is, of course, a cynical reduction of the Christian dogma, but it's not inaccurate. That was certainly not the kind of God I saw in my vision.

God told me that He had created the Earth for us, so that we could experience life fully. It was not designed as a morality test to be graded upon death.

If everything God was telling me was true, though, how did the Bible's authors get it so wrong?

God told me, simply, that if you tell people that something is free, no one will ever pay for it. That includes salvation. And what cathedrals are built by healing the sick or feeding the hungry? None. Cathedrals are built the same way any other worldly thing is built. Money.

Without cold hard cash, the Church would never have survived. The early Church leaders were no fools to this reality, so they rationalized their actions and did what they believed needed to be done. They distorted Jesus's words and his life story just enough to make them profitable. They did this not to get rich themselves, but for the sake of spreading Christianity in general.

One interesting bit of evidence that supports this theory comes from the Apostle Paul, often called "the Father of Christianity" because he authored most of the New Testament. Although he never actually met Jesus, Paul was a major figure in shaping the religion. Full disclosure, I've never been a big fan of Paul. Without his writings, women would be allowed to preach, there would be no New Testament argument against homosexuality, and so on. As such, I haven't read any of Paul's writings in over a decade; but about six months ago, a Christian friend posted a quote from Paul's second letter to the Corinthians on her Facebook wall. It read: "Even if we did think of the Messiah from a human point of view, we don't think of him that way anymore."[12]

That certainly got my attention! "Even if we *did* think of the Messiah from a *human point of view*, we don't think of him that way anymore." To me, this is literally an acknowledgement from Paul that he and the other early Christians knew that Jesus was just a man with a beautiful message, not a miracle-wielding demigod. And such an acknowledgment (from Paul, of all people) was staggering to me, because it seemed to confirm my hallucinogenic suspicions that the early Church leaders knew exactly what they were doing by inflating Jesus's supernatural persona.

I never asked my friend why on Earth she posted that quote, but I'm glad she did!

Despite a few voices within the early Christian community who objected, by making Christ's teachings mandatory (punishable by "eternal damnation"), raising money became easy. This was completely contrary to

Christ's actual teachings (both in the Bible and in my hallucination), but it worked. The Christian Church grew very large and very powerful, very quickly.

It's worth noting, God wasn't angry about any of this. In fact, He basically defended the early Christians. He insisted that the early Church leaders weren't malicious, but merely realistic (they became malicious during the Dark Ages, but that's another story). They only wanted Christ's teachings to survive in a world ruled by money, and in their defense, it did.

I had my misgivings, but again, God reiterated that none of these things were very important. He said that no one really believed in Christ just because "his mother was a virgin," but because they heard truth in Christ's message. The message had always been more powerful than the superstition, and true believers in Christ understood this.

God did acknowledge that there were people who focused on all the wrong things in the Bible. Mankind, in its endless egocentricity, often tries to "do God's work" for Him, as if He weren't powerful enough to do it for Himself. They pick verses here and there to support their local agendas. But while religion is clearly a pitfall for some, it is all part of the necessary fabric of God's complex Creation. Even the nuttiest of religious nut-jobs was just another piece of a much larger puzzle. In the end, as we say in the South, it all comes out in the wash.

I asked if this meant that God had intended for Christ's story to be distorted. He replied that He had not intended anything after the death of Christ. He accomplished His mission: to use Christ's life as a means to understand mankind, and to give Himself over to mankind so that we would no longer be separated from Him. What became of Christ's legend in the millennia that followed was more or less irrelevant to God.

God acknowledged, though, that it was not surprising that His presence on Earth would become a myth and ultimately a religion. He was *God*, after all. Any action He takes, even in human form, is bound to cause a few ripples in the space-time continuum.

In the end, God pressed me to understand that the Bible itself was merely a reflection of everything else in the Universe; it is neither pure good, nor pure evil. The constant human insistence that it must be one or the other does not make it so. In His words, "The Bible is what it is; just as I am what I am, and you are what you are."

This simple statement from God was actually quite profound for me.

A fundamental belief I had held for many years, and still hold, is that our desperate need for "identity" is the driving force behind most of our lives. It seems to develop immediately in childhood: Am I male or female? Am I parent or child? Teacher or student? Black or white? Loved or unloved? Rich or poor? Happy or sad? Healthy or handicapped? Right or wrong? Weak or strong? Am I good or am I evil? We think these answers will help us, yet we can so easily spend our entire lives searching for ourselves in such binary questions, and finding nothing. Why? The truth is, we are neither parent nor child; we are both. We are neither teacher nor student, but both. We are neither masculine or feminine, but both. Neither healthy nor handicapped, but both. Neither black nor white, but human. Neither good nor evil, but whole.

The challenge for me, in that moment, was this: why did I look at the Bible, or any religious text, and insist upon some kind of binary purity or simplicity? Perhaps it is because the religious right is so outspoken in its insistence that the Bible is perfect, despite its obvious theological conflicts and its occasionally meandering moral compass. Perhaps it is because the anti-theists of the far left are hell-bent on convincing us that all religion is poison. Either way, neither extreme ever felt right to me, so why was I still looking in such places to find answers?

What I was learning through this hallucination was that it was not necessary to throw the baby Jesus out with the holy bath water.

In a funny way, I felt willing to forgive the Bible for all the pain and confusion and illogic it had brought me all these years. And if I was capable of forgiving the Bible, perhaps I was capable of forgiving my father, and the people from my childhood church, and the random folks who slithered onto my Facebook threads every time I posted something political or religious. For that matter, maybe I was capable of truly forgiving God, and myself, for feeling so lost for so long.

None of these things were small feats, by any measure. The psychological work being done here on the subconscious level was astounding! Somehow, through everything God had told me, I felt freer than I had ever felt before. And maybe that was the sole purpose of this encounter with God to begin with.

PART IX: The Failsafe

Let me backtrack to something that deserves a little more attention: the issue of exactly what It was that I was communicating with. "God," yes, but exactly which part of Him/Her/It?

As I said before, God told me that He once existed as an external god, but through living and dying in human form (through "Christ") He tore Himself into countless pieces ("supernova"-style) and spread Himself across Creation, into mankind in particular, and became something else. He/She/It became a trillion-trillion-trillion tiny god particles, spread out across all living things. It was one such sliver of God, the tiny piece of Him that existed *within me*, that was communicating with me now.

There was an overwhelming sense of peace that came with this knowledge, because it confirmed that God was always there with me. Not only because He cared about my personal well-being, but because He was literally stuck in my head, experiencing everything I was experiencing. This might seem like some kind of invasion of privacy at first glance, but then you have to remember that we're all just a part of His Creation anyway, so it's more accurate to say that we're kind of stuck in *His* head. We are fundamentally inseparable from Him in this way (so, in practical terms, it would be like saying your right brain was invading the privacy of your left brain...which makes no sense).

Knowing that God was hanging around in my brain 24/7, I had a newfound sense of confidence. I realized that God was there, permanently, to act as the ultimate failsafe in case of emergency. In the event of utter distress (say, for example, a paralyzing fear of dental procedures), the tiny piece of God that belonged to me would override my senses and rescue me.

God confirmed this theory, as such.

He explained that He was effectively the part of the human brain that activated by necessity whenever the rest of the brain panicked or otherwise failed. That was His true gift to mankind when He made Himself a part of us. That's why His self-sacrifice was so great; He sacrificed Himself literally to protect us, which is where the notion of God (or Jesus) being our "savior" originated. In a way, it was literally true.

There is an expression in the Christian subculture that says, "God will never give you more than you can handle." It is derived from an actual Bible verse, 1 Corinthians 10:13, which says, "God is faithful, and he will not let you be tested beyond your strength." However, up until this precise moment in my life, that notion had proven to be complete bullshit. I had been so overwhelmed by emotional hardship at multiple points in my life that I had my faith knocked right out of me. I'm not just talking about a few sleepless nights; I'm talking about spurts of crippling depression, standing-on-a-chair-with-a-rope-around-my-neck kind of debilitation. For my money, that's literally the opposite of "handling" it. God gave me more than I could handle, and I'm willing to wager that most human beings of a certain age can recall a time or two where God gave them too much to handle, too.

The eternal optimist might say, "But we're still alive, so you obviously *did* handle whatever God threw at you." To which I would say two things: one, not all of us made it. Try explaining 1 Corinthians 10:13 to the loved ones of a suicide victim. And two, if surviving suicide is the litmus test for "handling" what God throws at you, God is a maniacal son of a bitch. There, I said it. That's not a God I'd want to meet.

Unfortunately, for many years, that was exactly the kind of God I was struggling to worship.

I was relatively young when I began to realize that the "God" I was subscribing to was weak and ineffective. He only answered prayers with silence. Silence that I mistook for being "mysterious" when, in actuality, it was just good old-fashioned silence. Worse still, that silent God made *me* feel weak: weak for needing Him so desperately to begin with (which I accepted and labeled as "humility"), weak for apparently failing Him so miserably (so as to warrant His silence, if not His wrath), and ultimately weak for continuing to worship Him despite His apparent lack of interest in me.

However, I didn't immediately jump to "God does not exist." I first went through a phase of believing that God must only "help those who help themselves" (a secular expression, but it didn't matter at the time).

I stopped turning to God for help and started searching for my own solutions. I eventually found a few self-destructive ways of "helping myself," the first of which was to face my anger, guilt and weakness head-on by employing a strange and bloody ritual called cutting.

If you are unfamiliar with cutting (or non-suicidal self-injury, NSSI[13]) it is the practice of self-inflicting wounds for the sake of physicalizing an emotional pain. It is not unlike the archaic Christian practice of flagellation, in which a subject punishes himself by whipping or flogging, meant to replicate the beating of Christ at the hands of the Romans just before the crucifixion. It was this ancient, ritualistic use of self-punishment that first gave me the idea to inflict wounds on myself as a way of "handling" emotional stress.

I didn't use whips or rods, but a simple serrated knife. It was swift and effective. I wasn't merely interested in the pain of the action; I wanted to see blood. Perhaps because I was never much of a crier and rarely had tears to confirm or defuse my emotional anxieties, I found an enormous release in seeing blood flowing out of my own body; it reassured me that I was *alive* and that everything I felt was real.

Sadly, this primitive practice truly made me feel better about things for nearly a decade.

In my defense, though I had no idea at the time, wounding the body actually triggers a chemical response in the brain, which I inadvertently exploited and eventually became addicted to. In scientific terms, it activates the body's opioid system, which floods the brain with pain-relieving and sedative neurotransmitters like dopamine and endorphins.[14] This creates a calming, almost euphoric effect on the mind and body, and the emotional turmoil seems to diminish. However, just like any other drug, over years of abuse, my self-medicating became compulsive, and without realizing it, I became addicted to it.

Granted, some people aren't just addicted to the endorphins, but are intentionally cutting exposed parts of the body (usually arms or legs) as a way of drawing attention to themselves, and ultimately asking for help. For me, though, it was the opposite. This was a secret ritual that I had invented on my own, and I thought it was a unique and creative solution for my inner troubles...and unanswered prayers. I primarily cut my thighs, so that no one would see the wounds.

I remember one night in college I had become so filled with self-loathing that I wanted to teach myself a particularly pointed lesson. I sat naked on the floor of my tiny apartment bathroom, and made one swift slice into my leg with a bit more force than I had probably intended. I was clever enough to know where the artery was in that part of the body, so as to be careful not to accidentally kill myself (which was never my intention with cutting), so I knew that I wasn't in danger of bleeding out, but I was also shocked by the amount of blood pouring out of me. My first response was to try and stop the bleeding, but then something else kicked in. It was probably the euphoric sensation of my brain chemistry at work, sending endorphins and dopamine to my aid, but I slipped into a state of ecstasy watching the dirty white tiles beneath me slowly turning red. I was witnessing my own life force literally spreading out all around me, taking over. My rage was gone. For a brief moment, my mind and my emotions felt balanced. And I sat there, peaceful, in a pool of my own blood, with only one thought: "God has forsaken me."

I started out a simple, amiable young man with a heart for the Lord, and this was where my humble search for God had led me. The search didn't completely end that night, mind you; I am nothing if not persistent. It took years before I would stop lamenting how God had abandoned me and simply learned to abandon Him instead.

Not surprisingly, it wasn't God who eventually led me out of this self-mutilation addiction. It was my own willpower and determination, albeit not under very noble circumstances. Truthfully, it was little more than vanity that pulled me out of these depths.

I had no idea that cutting was a well-documented psychological affliction. It wasn't until I hit rock bottom in college that I began seeing a therapist who told me that a substantial portion of the population (studies put the number around 17%[15]) have employed the use of cutting. Most of those people are young, adolescent or college age, just as I was at the time. When I became aware of these statistics, I instantly felt childish and pathetically trite.

The arguments against the use of NSSI as a means of self-medicating were boiled down to the notion that the usefulness of these tactics (much like the usefulness of other drugs) was limited to a temporary relief of emotional symptoms with no effect on the underlying emotional cause. While that argument was intellectually significant to me, it was not what ultimately led to my abandoning of the practice. I stopped cutting because too many other people were doing it, and I didn't want to be like other people. I wanted to be unique. So I stopped cutting, and stopped going to therapy.

Remember back in the beginning of my trip when God told me that I was incapable of trusting anyone else but myself? Well, this example from my late teens and early twenties exemplifies that.

While I eventually freed myself from the self-mutilation, I was still lost, and growing increasingly bitter about God's lack of action in my life.

The years after college, through most of my twenties, I was dealt a series of incredibly bad financial losses and business conundrums, year after year. "Bad luck," as most of my friends and family called it at the time. The events devastated me, financially and emotionally. No longer having NSSI in my bag of tricks, I fell into relying on marijuana to quiet my mind and numb my emotions. But in the end, like all drugs of this kind, weed only served as a tool of avoidance. I was only delaying the inevitable task of actually dealing with my emotional wreckage, rather than hiding from it.

The problem was, I didn't know how to actually deal with any of these things. I had never developed any resources for processing such difficulties. Whether it was "giving my problems over to God" or cutting or smoking weed, it was all the same. None of these things actually *dealt* with the complex emotional roots of my problems.

That lack of any healthy coping mechanism eventually led me to suicidal thoughts. It wasn't any one misfortune or emotional pitfall that triggered this, but a lifetime of unresolved, seemingly insurmountable sufferings.

Luckily for me, in the end, something always held me back from actually going through with it. It was a deep-rooted, undeniable will to live. In spite of everything, something in me always kicked in, saying, "Keep fighting. This is not the end."

That day, in the dentist's chair, the God in my head told me, "That voice was me."

This threw me for a loop. Once I had finally come to believe that God wasn't paying any attention (and that 1 Corinthians 10:13 was completely busted), here God was telling me that it was true. Or, at least, it was half true.

The verse says that God won't give you anything you can't handle. From my perspective, God had *consistently* overwhelmed me with misfortune.

God explained that the verse was simply misleading.

He claimed to make no promises as to whether or not we would be given "only so much as we could handle" throughout our lives on Earth. In fact, feeling overwhelmed against seemingly impossible odds was all part of the human experience He had intended for us.

Instead, He was promising that in those moments of desperation, when we felt completely submerged and alone, He'd be there, waiting for us, no matter what happens (death by suicide or not). He was our spiritual safety net, not necessarily our physical or emotional safety net, if that makes sense.

However, that's not to say that this spiritual safety net was strictly limited to the spiritual realm; it also had implications in the physical world. For example, I once met a guy who had fallen from a job site, from some three stories in the air. He broke almost every bone in his body, but survived. I asked him what went through his mind when he fell, and he told me that he blacked-out as soon as his body slipped into the open air. He woke up hours or maybe days later (I can't remember), with doctors busily trying to put him back together.

At the time, I thought to myself how clever the human body was for having a "safe mode" that simply turned your brain "off" before suffering catastrophic damages. The man told me that if He hadn't blacked out, his muscles would have attempted to brace for the impact of the fall, which likely would have killed him. So, it was his mind "shutting down" that saved his life.

I thought little more about this man's harrowing story until years later, in that dentist's chair, when God told me that He was our failsafe that shutdown the system during emergencies. If the emergency resulted in a person dying, God was there to guide them to the other side. Otherwise, if the person survived, God was typically unseen.

It was this kind of major trauma that induced God to trigger the psychological self-destruct button. While the body was capable of minor self-regulation (for example, the brain's opioid release after minor cuts), it was only at the extremes that God's failsafe system truly went into action, usually at the border between life and death.

For a select few, apparently myself included, life circumstances are such that we need to access God earlier in our journeys than our deathbeds. He can appear to people, but generally, He does not communicate in this way. After all, the goal has always been that people should find God in their own unique ways (as discussed in Parts IV and V of this chapter).

For me, meeting God was a combination of ongoing emotional turmoil, a spiritual crisis, a deep-rooted phobia and, most notably, a shortage of oxygen to my brain (which I'll discuss further at the end of this book). I can't explain why I didn't merely black out, or why God chose to communicate with me, but I'm thankful that He did. As inspiring, entertaining and enlightening as it all was to me, more than anything, it was reassuring.

No matter what, we are safe, and we are not alone.

PART X: Bible School

God and I covered a lot of ground, but tended to linger on religious themes, probably because He was, you know, God.

Here are a few snapshots from the conversations we had pertaining to Biblical stories/dogma, for any of you who are interested in such things. I won't spend a lot of time on them here because they were merely points of curiosity during my hallucination, and as such, they aren't entirely relevant to the main thrust of this book. Nevertheless...

The Garden of Eden

Full disclosure: I've always thought the Creation story in Genesis was kind of dumb. Poisoned apples, talking snakes, strategically placed fig leaves, a flying baby with a flaming sword that prevents people from reentering the Garden...I mean, really? It boggles my mind that there are grown adults who take this stuff seriously (says the guy writing a book about what God told him at the dentist's office).

God was pretty clear that the creation story was a primitive allegory strung together by early humans to simply suggest the existence of a Creator. It was not a literal account, although some of the *themes* were based on truth—namely that God created mankind in His image and that humans chose existential knowledge over immortality (in Genesis, the "Tree of Knowledge" over the "Tree of Life").

To recapitulate: Adam and Eve were not actual people, there was no talking snake, no poisoned apple, no angel-bouncer with a combustible cutlass.

Frankly, this came as a relief to me because for years I couldn't help being grossed out about "Mr. Adam and Mrs. Eve" having to populate the entire planet from scratch, with no one else to have sex with...which meant that after they had kids...what happened? They either started having sex with the kids, or the kids started having sex with each other. Either way— Ew! Granted, only Biblical literalists have to swallow that disgusting pill, but still. It kinda taints the whole story a little, doesn't it?

Anyway, unless you thought the Bible was originally written in English, none of this should come as a complete shock. In the original Hebrew text, "Adam" is not a proper noun, but a generic noun; it literally means "mankind."[16] Also, "Eve" (or "hawwah" in Hebrew) is not a name; it means "source of life" (referring to childbearing)[17]. With these nouns misrepresented as proper names, it's easy to see why there has been some confusion.

Other Old Testament Stories

In a nutshell, all of the Old Testament stories were either completely allegorical (like the story of Adam & Eve) or very loosely based on real events (like the story of Noah's Ark).

For example, God told me that there were many "great floods" documented in nearly every ancient religion, not because the entire globe was ever simultaneously flooded, but because devastating floods (and tsunamis, etc.) are common Earth science events, regardless of where anyone lives. There was never an "ark," Noah and his family were completely fictional, and rainbows did, in fact, exist prior to this particular flood story. (If you're not familiar, the story ends with God creating a rainbow for the first time. #SpoilerAlert)

Another example is my namesake, Joshua, who has many heroic tales in the Old Testament of winning battles against impossible odds. He was, according to the God in my head, a great military leader. But, all of the stories about his battles were written hundreds of years after they took place, and were inflated to epic proportions.

These examples go on and on: Sodom & Gomorrah, Joseph's adventures getting into Egypt, Moses's adventures getting out of Egypt, David & Goliath. Others were full-fledged allegories, like the Tower of Babel, Samson & Delilah, Jonah & the Whale, etc.

I apologize in advance to any Jews or Old Testament scholars who were hoping I'd say anything profound. But none of this is either radical or unique. Most people who read these stories today do not take them at face value.

That said, nothing in my vision indicated that these stories are worthless or trite in any way. To the contrary, God seemed to have a fondness for them as morality lessons (not unlike *Aesop's Fables* or, perhaps more appropriately, *Grimm's Fairy Tales*).

Leviticus and Deuteronomy

If you're unfamiliar, two of the most controversial books that Christians have to deal with today are the Old Testament chestnuts Leviticus and Deuteronomy. These books contain all of the ancient laws of the Israelites.

In addition to the basic civil laws that you might expect to find (such as laws against murder, thievery and rape), the books also cover more bizarre "sins" (like eating pork or shellfish, mixing fabrics in clothing, and women wearing pants). Because of the latter, Christian literalists are put in an awkward position today. They either concede that some of the old laws are no longer necessary, or they insist that they're all valid even though some of them are virtually impossible (if not illegal) to follow today.

To truly follow the old laws, you'd have to murder your children if they ever spoke back to you.[18] You'd have to kill any homosexual you encountered.[19] You'd have to leave town and never return if you have sex with your wife while she's menstruating.[20] The list goes on and on. Needless to say, you'd have to be a sociopath in order to observe all of these laws precisely as they are written. In my experience, even the most fundamentalist Christians know that they must contextualize such verses, or hypocritically cherry-pick which laws to observe and which to ignore.

To put it in perspective, had the ancient Israelites also recorded their medical techniques, weapon manufacturing methods or farming practices, those documents would also be completely useless today, except for their historical value. It is therefore bizarre that anyone takes these ancient civil codes, hygiene practices and other local customs as relevant to society today.

In my hallucination, God was not attached to any of these laws. They served their purpose in their day, creating civil order in ancient times. As far as He was concerned, that was the end of it.

Angels

There are a handful of dubious references to "angels" in the Bible (a.k.a. cherubim or seraphim), but the jury is still out on what their deal really is. Most people go with the pop-culture version—a guardian angel in a long white robe, with two dove-like wings, maybe a harp. Sadly, there are no references to "guardian angels" or harps in the Bible, but the Good Book does offer a few other trippy descriptions.

Isaiah says angels have six wings.[21] Daniel says they've got no wings, but bronze bodies, lightning for faces and fire for eyes.[22] In Ezekiel, they're downright monstrous, with bodies of interlocking "whirling wheels" covered in eyeballs, with four human and/or animal faces.[23] Needless to say, Biblically speaking, angels could be damn near anything, which is probably why very few Christians talk about them very much on a serious level.

So what did God tell me about angels? Cue the drum roll: He said they don't exist. (Now cue the *Price Is Right* loser tuba.)

God said that whenever humans interacted with their own unique "God-particle" (like the one I was presently chatting with), they saw God however their subconscious minds chose to see Him (as explained in Part I of this chapter). For me, I saw a mirror image of myself. For others, they saw "angels"...or, in Ezekiel's case, a bunch of spinning eyeball-wheels. (I can only assume Ezekiel was on nitrous oxide at the time.)

Some people see a *group* of angels, some see Jesus, or the Virgin Mary, or a bright light, or a burning bush, a dead relative, an animal guide, an extraterrestrial alien or literally anything else imaginable. Throughout history, all of these visions were merely that small piece of God that existed within each person, manifesting itself however each person chose or needed to see It.

Perhaps a more positive way of expressing all this is to say that angels *do* exist, but that they aren't really "angels," they're just another manifestation of God Himself; a form assigned by the subconscious minds of the people witnessing Him.

This theory also explains why angels are described so differently throughout the Bible. Just sayin'.

I guess this is both good news and bad news for conservative Christians. The bad news is that the Bible isn't incredibly accurate, but the good news is that the tasks of "guardian angels," and other kinds of angels, are actually fulfilled by God Himself! So...all's well that ends well.

The (Non-Tasmanian) Devil

Most Christians believe that the Devil (a.k.a. "Satan" or "Beelzebub") was once an angel named "Lucifer" who turned on God and left Heaven with a crew of other angelic mutineers (who were later called "demons"). This all theoretically happened in the very beginning of time, before or during the Garden of Eden, when Satan appeared as a serpent and caused man to sin for the first time. Then, the Devil somehow gained control over the Earth and continues to wreak spiritual havoc to this day. One passage in the New Testament goes so far as to call him "the god of this world."[24]

However, surprisingly, there isn't a lot of evidence in the Bible to validate this narrative, particularly in the Old Testament, which is why Jews don't hold similar beliefs about the Devil. Historians and scholars can only speculate as to how the early Christians got from point A to point B, but even if you choose to accept the story, it doesn't make a lot of sense.

If God is all-powerful, why didn't He just squash "Lucifer" immediately, and prevent him from taking over the world? Better yet, if God is all-knowing, shouldn't He have seen Lucifer's rebellion coming before He even created him? Why would He have let any of this happen to begin with?

The popular Christian answer is that mankind needed free will, in order to be able to choose to love God, rather than being forced to love God simply because they had no alternative. The Devil, therefore, provided humanity the necessary option to either follow God or not.

The problem with this, of course, is that it makes God's plan for humankind reliant on Satan. God used Satan in order to give us free will. In which case, the Devil wasn't really rebelling against God, he was fulfilling God's plan. So is Satan really a bad guy or not?

If you've been keeping up with the themes of my hallucination so far, you probably already know where I'm going with this.

According to the God in my head, there was a classic *Scooby-Doo* ending on this particular tale. Behind the pitchfork and the scary mask, Satan was no devil at all, but none other than...God Himself. ("And I would've gotten away with it, if it weren't for you and that stupid dentist.")

That's right. The truth was that God and the Devil were two halves of a whole, just like Yin and Yang, love and fear, good and evil.

There was no evil creature trolling the Earth looking to ruin people's lives. No demon ever hijacked anyone's mind or possessed their body; some people just have diagnosable mental disorders. Satan wasn't leading men into temptation with the bodies of beautiful women; men were just designed by God with hormones, which guaranteed the survival of the human species. Lucifer did not trick any gay or lesbian couple into falling in love; they were just designed by God to be attracted to the same sex, which will help slow down overpopulation and save the human species from extinction some day. Just sayin'.

These examples could go on and on, but I think you get the point. There was only one force in the Universe, and that force was God. No other entity existed that threatened God's authority in any way, either in Heaven or on Earth.

That said, God also told me that some people needed to see good and evil separated in order to make sense of the world around them. These were people who struggled to accept that life was designed to be complex, diverse and difficult. For them, God appeared as two separate entities, both "God" (the good) and "the Devil" (the bad). In this way, those who needed such structure could find it—a religious system with clearly marked labels, like Christianity. Other men and women, those who could grasp the vastness and inherent duality of God, traditionally found other faith traditions that better suited them, like Taoism, the Baha'i or Buddhism.

A friend of mine with a philosophy degree who read an early draft of this book insisted that such ideas were not unique (citing Taoism, specifically). However, to me at the time, this concept was utterly radical.

Heaven and Hell

Perhaps one of the most glaring principles that came out of my hallucination was the complete obliteration of Heaven and Hell. I touched on this subject earlier, describing how I witnessed Jesus preaching that Heaven and Hell were merely "states of consciousness," not literal afterlife destinations. That is, righteous living is capable of manifesting "Heaven on Earth," while wickedness often results in "Hell on Earth."

When I asked God directly whether or not such places existed, He was very forthcoming. To demonstrate how blunt this conversation was, allow me to dictate it, verbatim:

Me: "Do Heaven or Hell exist?"

God: "No."

That was it.

However, it's worth restating what God told me regarding the theology behind Heaven and Hell. It basically originated from the early Christian "organizers" (as God called them), the same ones who turned Jesus's life story into a superhero adventure, decades after the man had died. The idea of a scenario in which Christians (and *only* Christians) were infinitely rewarded while non-Christians, no matter how innocent or noble, were brutally punished in the afterlife, was the perfect recipe for creating an urgent, unchallengeable and ultimately sustainable religion. Heaven and Hell also satisfy our basic human desire for justice and fairness—the notion that in the end, even if you can't see it happen, everyone gets what they deserve. This was all much more appealing than the generic "underworld" doctrines of the day (namely, the Jewish afterlife, a neutral place where all souls end up, called "Sheol," similar to the Greek "Hades").

In my vision of Christ's life, Jesus once asked the people he was preaching to if they believed in a "God of judgment" who would prepare "a torturous pit" for his own children if they disobeyed Him. In a line very similar to the traditional text,[25] Jesus debunked such a theory, saying even the most criminal of men understand the love that a parent has for a child. To paraphrase as best I can, Jesus said, "If your child asks you for an apple, would you give him a viper? Of course not. How much greater then is God's love for His children? Would our Father hear His children cry out, and comfort them by throwing them into fire? Of course not, because God's love is greater than ours; it is unconditional."

Preach on, subconscious-Jesus, preach on.

The Book of Revelation

The last book of the Bible is an extremely bizarre description of the end of the world (the apocalypse, or "Armageddon"); it is called The Book of Revelation. While exiled on an island at the end of his life, the Apostle John allegedly wrote the book after having a hallucination in which Jesus came to him and showed him these dark events. John saw God's throne room in Heaven, followed by things like stars falling to the Earth, the sun going dark, the moon and the oceans turning to blood, most of the population dying in nasty ways, and then, my personal favorite, a prostitute riding a seven-headed monster![26] Obviously, most people (even fundamentalists) believe that this stuff is all symbolic. The problem with the allegory is that it's so vague that every generation believes the "signs of the apocalypse" are describing their own current events.

Well, God had a massive amount of apocalyptic teaching to offer me the day I met Him. We spent a lot of time talking about Revelation, probably because I've always been so curious about it. Half of what He told me felt completely random at the time, but when I compared His words to the actual Book of Revelation, eerily, it all kind of lined up.

Unfortunately, much like the details of the Gospel story, a full analysis of Revelation would be a book unto itself. As much as I'd like to share all of those pseudo-psychedelic interpretations with you, I will resist and simply break down a few key elements.

God said that the Book of Revelation was not about the end of the world at all. Instead, it was about the end of *Christianity* (or, at least, the end of Christ's original teachings).

Let me explain.

According to the God in my head, unlike most books in the Bible, the Book of Revelation was actually written by the man who the Church claims wrote it, the apostle John.

120

John was the last surviving disciple of Jesus. As such, he watched as the first Christian churches began to arise, all of which were led by men and women who had never actually known Christ. In an attempt to gain new converts, these early churches began to skew Christ's teachings, literally writing their own gospels. Christ's original message of God's universal love and acceptance was replaced by the exclusive brand of Christianity that we have today (one in which God favors only Christians, and plans to incinerate any who refuse to follow Christ's teachings). And Jesus's life as a man was replaced by his life as a *Superman*.

John, one of Jesus's closest friends, was outraged by the organization's bid to hijack the true message of Christ. He fought against it as best as he could, but John was out matched by the growing strength of the new Church. Nonetheless, after he was exiled to the island of Patmos, John wrote Revelation as a sort of final volley against these awful new teachings, and the spiritual elitism that he believed they fostered. It was also an eerily accurate prophecy about what would happen to the future Church under these new doctrines.

John knew that he was too late, but wrote the book in pure defiance.

He opens his treatise with this: "Blessed is the one who reads aloud the words of this prophecy, and blessed are those who hear, and who keep what is written in it, for the time is soon."

God told me that John literally meant *soon*, as in now, immediately, with no time left to spare. The destruction of Christianity was not just at the doorstep, it had already entered the house, and the fate of the new Christian Church was already beginning to unfold.

The first few chapters are an open attack on six of the seven early churches that existed at the time—the churches of Ephesus, Smyrna, Pergamum, Thyatira, Sardis and Laodicea. He calls them out one by one, accusing them of "abandoning love," being "synagogues of Satan," "lukewarm" with only "reputations of being alive" though they were truly dead.

The only church that John praises is the church at Philadelphia. Although he says that this church has "little power," John tells them that Jesus is pleased with their efforts because they have "kept his works," honoring the message Jesus had given them, which was (in John's words) an "open door, which no one is able to shut."[27] This "open door" refers to the universal doctrine that Christ preached, unconditional love and salvation for *all* (not just for Christians).

Everything God told me about the meaning of Revelation boils down to these seven churches. The entire book was a warning, written directly to them. This is why the number seven turns up over and over in the writing (seven torches, seven seals, seven trumpets, seven bowls, seven angels, seven plagues, a beast with seven heads, and so on). This alone should give you the gist of the interpretation I was given, without having to get into all the gory details.

However, since everyone I tell about this always wants to know, I'll tell you one other small detail: the identity of the infamous "Antichrist."

The Antichrist is described in Revelation as an ally to Satan himself, a "beast" identified by the number 666. This character gets a lot of media attention, particularly whenever Christians don't like a progressive politician (again, every generation thinks the Book of Revelation is written about them). Like most people, I was desperate to know who the Antichrist was, or if he was supposed to represent a real person at all. So here it is. God's answer.

God told me that the Antichrist was none other than...*the Apostle Paul.*

Record scratch!

I know, right? Look, don't shoot the messenger; I'm just a psychedelic journalist, man. I'm only half joking when I say that this is some serious *Da Vinci Code* shit, and that I'm kind of paranoid that the Illuminati are going to jump out and Tom Hanks me any second...but yes, we're talking about *that* Paul: Paul of Tarsus, Saint Paul, the author of almost the entire New Testament, the "Father of Christianity".

According to my vision, Paul was the Antichrist, and John hated him with a fiery passion.

Paul was obviously a major leader of the early Church, despite the fact that he never met Jesus. To John, he was the figurehead that represented the Church's move to rewrite Jesus's teachings, making salvation conditional upon belief in the Bible, with eternal consequences in

the afterlife. This was literally the opposite of Christ's message, makii
the *anti*-Christ, according to John.

Paul was, after all, the man who theorized that God might have
created some people simply to throw them into Hell, and that if so, we
humans had no right to question it.[28] Obviously, if Jesus truly taught that
God's love was unconditional, such a monstrous theology would have been
downright evil in the eyes of John (or any other of Jesus's true followers).

In Revelation, John says that the Antichrist has horns like a lamb,
but talks like a dragon,[29] meaning Paul seems to be like Christ, but is
actually like the Devil. The Antichrist will also exercise authority over the
"seven-headed beast" and cause the world to worship the beast,[30] meaning
Paul's authority over the seven churches will lead to people worshipping the
Church rather than worshipping Christ. Most damningly, John says that
the "seven-headed beast" will "go to war against the saints and conquer
them,"[31] meaning the seven churches will destroy the teachings of Christ
and the teachings of his true disciples, and they will win.

At the end of the story, it's not surprising that John predicts that
the Antichrist and the seven-headed beast will be thrown into Hell with
Satan himself.

Furthermore, he reiterates Jesus's universal message of acceptance
one last time, writing defiantly: "Let the one who is thirsty come; let the
one who desires take the water of life without price."

The words "without price" are important. To take the gift of
salvation you must give nothing—no amount of money, no amount of
good deeds, no amount of prayer, no amount of belief—the gift is utterly
free. Indeed, the doorway to the Kingdom of Heaven is wide open, for all
who wish to enter.

Fill my glass up with "the water of life," John...I'll drink to that.

PART XI: SIN

Upon asking about the issue of sin, I expected God to tell me that it didn't exist. After all, if the Devil wasn't real, and Hell wasn't real, it seemed logical to assume that "sin" itself was just another manipulative device conjured up to organize and control the masses.

To my surprise, however, God told me that this was not the case. At least not entirely.

Sin is an interesting proposition in the Bible, both theologically and linguistically (at least for English speakers). Contemporary Christians like to say that the word "sin" means "to miss the mark," because in the original Hebrew, the word "sin" was frequently used in the context of a spear or arrow missing a target.[32] The problem with this definition is that there are many different Hebrew words translated en masse as "sin" for the English translation of the Bible. While some of those words were in the context of "missing the mark," most were contextually closer to "wicked acts," "transgressions against God," or "guilt-worthy moral offenses."[33] The latter, most normative, definition of sin is the definition that God refuted in my hallucination, basically preferring the former instead. That is, despite the linguistic/historic evidence above, God told me that sin was, in fact, closer to simply "missing the mark."

Complicating the issue even further, God told me that morality itself was a moving target. One man's sin (and, thereby, one man's morality) may not be exactly the same as another man's. This was not some radical new approach to morality; it's been around a long time. It's called "moral relativism."

Most Christians hate (and I mean *hate*) the idea of moral relativity. It undermines their authority over morality by essentially saying that every person is responsible for deciding his or her own moral code, as opposed to having a God decide those things for everyone. They'll argue extremes like, "If morality is relative, then psychopaths can just say that murder isn't a sin at all, because for them, they have no moral compass that tells them it's wrong." In a sense, that's true. On an extreme level, someone with a diagnosable mental disability may not be able to reason for himself, therefore he cannot be held liable for his amoral actions. Our legal system certainly caters to that hypothesis and, according to my hallucination, so does God.

God told me that it was some people's fate in life to be born disfigured or handicapped, either physically or mentally. Those poor souls have a much harder road to travel than the majority of us able-bodied humans. However, one thing those souls are not subject too is additional punishment or judgment based on moral choices that they are, literally, incapable of making.

For most observers, this logic probably makes sense on its own. However, to help Christians understand it, allow me to suggest that it falls under the same pseudo-Biblical logic as God allowing babies into Heaven, even if they die before being baptized or otherwise converted to Christianity.

If you're non-Christian, babies going to Hell probably sounds ridiculous, and perhaps offensive, but let me clarify. Generally speaking, Christians believe that all humans are born with sin. That is, we are sinful by nature, thusly separated from God as soon as we enter the world in human form. Unfortunately, this puts infants in some danger because if they die prior to accepting Jesus as their savior, theoretically, they go to Hell. There is no specific loophole for babies (or mentally handicapped people, for that matter) written into the Bible. So, over the centuries, different Christian denominations have created their own loopholes.

Catholics believe that if you have a priest sprinkle water over the baby, the child will be protected from Hell until it grows old enough to make religious choices on its own. Well-studied Protestants invoke something they call "the Age of Accountability", which uses a handful of loosely written Bible verses to suggest that God understands that children are incapable of knowing good from evil, which theoretically excuses them from His wrath in the afterlife.[34] Some may stretch this logic further to cover mentally handicapped adults, although there is certainly no Biblical justification to do so.

All of this, of course, is the horrifying nonsense that Atheists have a field day with. Nevertheless, I use it as an example of how Christians already have similar beliefs in place regarding the limits of our moral liability.

Extreme examples aside, Christians are still uncomfortable putting morality in the hands of each individual person. Yet, the best examples of moral relativism are found in the pages of the Bible itself.

Murder, for example, is one of the Ten Commandments (the Bible's most rudimentary list of dos and don'ts), yet God ordains the murder of countless people throughout the Old Testament. The Bible's real message, therefore, is that murder is wrong, except when God says it's right. In other words, murder is *morally relative* to its surrounding circumstances (not by my authority, but by the Bible's).

Another favorite example of this is, "Thou shalt not lie," another of the Ten Commandments. Generally speaking, sure, lying is a sin. But practically speaking, if your mother asks whether or not her hideous sweater makes her look fat, is the morally correct response to tell her the *absolute truth*? Or is it better to lie and tell her she looks great?

If we assume "white lies" don't count, let's raise the stakes: imagine it's 1943, you're living on the border of France and you're hiding Jewish refugees in your attic. Nazi soldiers kick down your door and demand to know whether or not you're harboring Jews. Do you follow the Bible's black-and-white moral directive and tell them the absolute truth? Or do you break the Bible's law and lie to the Nazis to protect the Jews? If you think it's better to lie in order to save the refugees in the attic, congratulations, you are a moral relativist! Your perception of right and wrong depends on the circumstances, not on the letter of the law itself.

This puts the responsibility of morality precariously in our own hands, but God told me that this responsibility was part of every man's task in life. For this purpose, He equipped us with brains capable of complex reasoning. Any dog can be trained to follow simple rules, but only the Divine Species can know "morality". It's not about memorizing a list of offenses, it's about understanding yourself and understanding the world around you.

Why can't Christians just embrace moral relativism, you ask? The short answer is that if they did, they'd be pulling on a thread that would unravel their entire religion. The Bible must be "absolute truth," otherwise morality would be in the hands of humans, not God, and Christianity itself would become inconsequential. Christians are not okay with that.

If you agree that lying, for example, is sometimes morally better than telling the truth, on whose authority do you make that judgment? The Bible says not to lie, but using your own moral judgment you decide you know better? You can see what a slippery slope this is for Christians.

It gets even more slippery the higher the stakes are, or the grayer the moral area is. When is murdering someone the morally correct thing to do? Never? Only in extreme cases of self-defense? What about preemptive military strikes? Is pulling the plug on a stroke victim "murder"? What about abortion? Where are the lines drawn, and who's drawing them?

The Bible, in its ancient vagueness, can be used to argue all sides of these debates. Christian believers are therefore thrust, kicking and screaming, into moral relativism even as they claim to believe in "absolute truth." The inherent hypocrisy of it all is one of the many banes of many non-Christian.

In this part of our conversation, God told me there was little absolute truth in the Universe, if any at all, especially from our limited perspective as human beings.

When it came to sin, God told me that "wicked behavior" was relative to each person, based on each person's own unique life story and how their minds, bodies and spirits processed worldly things. It is our personal experiences and conditions that make certain acts "wrong" for us, individually. For example, alcohol is not inherently sinful, yet, for an alcoholic, it would be a "sin" to drink. That's because an alcoholic's life and well-being are heavily compromised by the alcohol in ways that do not apply to non-alcoholics.

Sin certainly isn't limited to addiction, though. For example, lying, cursing, stealing, and unmarried sex are not fundamentally "wrong" in and of themselves. Under the right conditions, they may be right.

The general rule is that any behavior that is destructive (either to oneself or to others) is sinful. Any behavior that is constructive, therefore, is righteous. God acknowledged that this kind of anti-absolutism was much more difficult than simply having a "rule book" that makes these decisions for you. Making your own decisions is hard...but then, the most fulfilling paths in life are rarely the easiest to navigate.

Jesus himself confirmed all of this when he was asked which of the old laws was the most important. He replied with "the Great Commandment," which was to love God with all your heart and to love your neighbor as yourself. He said, "All the laws and prophets hang on these two commandments."[35]

Some of the Bible's laws are perfectly valid today, in which case there is no reason to ignore them. It is hard to imagine any circumstance under which certain actions could ever be morally justified: rape, incest, genocide, and slavery, for example. (Although the Bible condones slavery about 150 times, but I digress.) The point is, to accurately address every possible scenario of "right and wrong" would take volumes of books, which is the precise reason that entire libraries are dedicated to legal texts in our country alone, and why the Jewish Talmud takes a lifetime to study. The Bible is not exceptional in this way; despite its impressive length, it is no match for all the world's moral complexities, past, present and future.

The line between right and wrong can be precariously thin at times, and the burden of finding it is not in ancient platitudes but in daily decision making. This incredible, turbulent, lifelong challenge is very much a part of what it means to be human. To understand what is right for you, and what is wrong for you, is rudimentary to understanding yourself. When you get it wrong, you "sin," betraying yourself and the people around you. God told me that there is no external punishment for such actions, per se, but that the repercussions of such "sins" were their own punishment. Prolonged exposure to sinful behavior results in creating a sort of Hell for yourself here on Earth, just as perpetual righteousness results in building up "the Kingdom of Heaven" all around you. This was the true message God was attempting to convey to me in my hallucination, and the true message Jesus attempted to convey to the world two thousand years ago.

Despite the fact that all of this information felt revelatory at the time, I had known it deep in my subconscious since I was a child.

When I was very young, perhaps four or five years old, my parents took me to a buffet restaurant (buffet restaurants were very popular in the South in those days). I wasn't tall enough to see the food on the buffet line, or strong enough to hold the heavy, ceramic plate by myself. So my father walked alongside me, carrying the plate and narrating which foods were available above. However, like most children, I was very curious and desperately wanted to either see or feel the food for myself.

Feeling food is a desire that most adults abandon, but in the mind of a child, the impulse is palpable.

There was no chance of me actually seeing the buffet given my height, but my arms were just long enough to reach up to the counter and feel around. My father swatted my hands away from the ledge, in the way that parents often ruined everything. Dad was, for the most part, successful in thwarting my efforts. After a few swats, he got very stern with me. He told me that there were open burners on the ledge above and that if I touched them I would be injured. For this reason, it was especially important that I obey him.

Now you probably see where the story is going. As soon as my father turned away, I reached up again and placed my palm squarely onto an open stovetop. My subsequent wailing probably ruined dinner for about a hundred people.

The key part of this story is that my father didn't punish me after I burned my hand. While he may have been disappointed with me for disobeying him, he was mostly just concerned for my well-being. He treated my wound as best he could and tried to soothe and comfort me until the pain subsided.

There was no need to punish me further; the act itself was clearly punishment enough. Instead, my father merely reiterated the importance of trusting him and assured me that he wasn't creating arbitrary rules to limit my experiences. He was only trying to protect me against actions that he knew would be painful.

This is precisely the way God explained "sin" to me in my hallucination.

PART XII: PRAYER & SUFFERING

I didn't know that I looked Jewish until I moved to Manhattan. I had no Jewish friends as a kid in the South because, frankly, there weren't many Jews down there. However, upon moving north of the Mason-Dixon, I was immediately taken in by God's Chosen People, probably because they thought I was one of them. My name is Joshua, I have curly dark hair and a generous nose, I'm an anxious person with a sensitive stomach, pork and shellfish disagree with me, I call my mother at least once a week; I'm practically Jewish.

Anyway, one thing I instantly observed was that my Jewish friends were not nearly as religious as my Christian friends. In fact, most were openly Agnostic or Universalist, admittedly Jewish only in heritage, not by faith (two separate aspects of Judaism, though not mutually exclusive). Coming from a Southern Baptist world, where evangelism is considered critical to one's faith, this non-religious group of "religious people" totally confused me.

One girl I dated in college celebrated the major Jewish holidays and could recite a number of traditional prayers in Hebrew, but when I asked her what the prayers meant in English, she had no idea. She had only learned them phonetically.

I asked another Jewish friend if they were actively waiting for the Messiah to come (assuming that Jesus was not the Messiah, of course), and she looked at me as if I were insane.

Eventually, I worked up the nerve to ask an older Jewish woman, whom I had become friendly with in New York, to explain why so many Jewish people were seemingly so non-spiritual. She chuckled at first, but then told me that she believed the prevalence of Atheism and Agnosticism in the Jewish community was a direct result of the Holocaust. I remember her saying to me, "Imagine you had to watch as everyone you ever knew – your parents, your children, your spouse, your neighbors, your friends – were all rounded up, enslaved and murdered simply because they believed in the same God as you." Despite their constant prayers, God's 'Chosen People' were slaughtered by the millions. The survivors were mostly scattered overseas where they became stigmatized and rejected again. Then she asked, "Would you still put your faith in such a god?"

She acknowledged that there were still Jews devoted to their faith today, but obviously she was not one of them. Instead, she honored her heritage by remembering the traditions of Judaism, through which she found wisdom and comfort, but nothing more.

Her words were unshakable to me. I knew she was right. If I had to endure anything close to such extremes at the hands of my God, I would have assumed that He didn't exist. It wasn't long after that conversation that fate dealt me a series of hard knocks, and the lack of response from the Almighty – after years of patiently waiting, desperate to hear His voice – I was driven into Agnostic nomadism myself.

However, before I confide in you exactly what God told me about earthly suffering and the power of prayer, let me preface this by saying that the issue of prayer, specifically, is a sensitive one for me. Despite the evidence to the contrary, I am of the opinion that prayer is one of the most beneficial aspects of faith. It seems to provide two great services. First, in order to pray in times of need or thanksgiving, one is forced into a practice of active self-reflection. This mere act of organizing one's own thoughts and emotions seems to be profoundly beneficial in and of itself, bringing intellectual order to emotional chaos. Secondly, this act of self-reflection is often a catalyst for releasing many of the mind's burdens, resulting in a mental state not totally dissimilar to the common meditation practices of Eastern religions, which I find equally rewarding.

Granted, using prayer to hand one's problems over to God may also produce a special kind of delusion, unique to religious folk, a feeling of holy protection against all odds. It certainly had that effect on me as a younger man, resulting in a few harsh crashes into reality.

This point cannot be more clearly articulated than the Holocaust example provided above. However, for the sake of the Christians who might be tempted to exempt themselves from such logic, as it does not directly pertain to Christianity, allow me to call your attention to a minor hero in the Southern Baptist history book, a turn-of-the-century missionary named Lottie Moon.

Lottie spent most of her life as a Southern Baptist missionary in China.[36] The story goes that she was helping spread the "Good News" by feeding a multitude of starving Chinese people when the mission's resources became overwhelmed. There was not enough food to feed all of the starving people. The organization had fallen into debt back home in the States, so they were unable to send any additional aid. Without telling her fellow missionaries, Lottie gave away all of her own food, as well as her income, in order to help as many people as possible. When the others discovered what she had done, they pleaded with her, but she insisted that she had been put there to do God's work, and that God would provide for her needs just as the Bible promised He would![37] Lottie died of starvation soon after.

In her honor, the Southern Baptist Church now holds an annual fundraising drive (called "The Lottie Moon Offering") that benefits Southern Baptist missionaries around the world.

Despite the clever public relations spin, to me this is a fantastic demonstration of the limits of prayer's power.

Religious folks like to suggest that God always answers prayers, even when it seems like His response goes against our own interests. That's fine for quelling the mild or moderate pains of life, I suppose, but it's pretty difficult to use that logic to justify poor Lottie's case. You could argue that it was simply "God's will" that Lottie should die in order to, say, start up a yearly donation drive, but that can't explain every missionary's death, let alone the countless unanswered prayers familiar to any of us who have ever hung hope on such things.

Beyond all this, the Christian idea of prayer simply makes no sense.

If God is all-knowing[38] and unchanging[39], as the Bible repeatedly says He is, the concept of prayer doesn't work.

Imagine you have some rare disease and you're dying. You pray that God will save your life. Now, because God is all-knowing, He already knows whether or not you will live or die, and because He is unchanging, there is no amount of praying that could change His mind. Therefore, your fate is predetermined and your prayers are irrelevant. (I won't get into a full discussion regarding predestination; it's a long and paradoxical issue that doesn't really affect us. I only mention it here because of how it affects the traditional notion of prayer.)

The only real way prayer could be relevant is if God is either not all-knowing or, at the very least, not unchanging. And no Christian is about to suggest either. If they did, the entire concept of who and what God is would be in jeopardy for them.

Take it or leave it, but in my hallucination, God told me He doesn't rearrange human destinies based on prayer. Sorry for this bad news, everyone.

He said that if you are destined to be hit by a bus next Thursday, no matter how hard you pray about it, the bus is coming. It's not about whether or not you deserve to be hit by a bus, or whether or not you prayed hard enough to justify God moving the bus on your behalf. The harsh reality is that humans are susceptible to basic statistics. That is, some of us are inevitably destined to be hit by buses. Christians, Jews, Hindus, Buddhists and Atheists alike—we all have the same statistical odds of being hit by buses.

Harsher still, statistically speaking, some of us will be murdered, raped, drowned, burned alive, tortured and maimed. Some parents will know the death of their children. Likewise, some children will grow up without parents. On and on such horrible scenarios could be laid out, just as positive and beautiful scenarios could be. All of these things, good and bad, are randomly distributed across the human population on a bell curve. That is, the vast majority of people will have life experiences filled with relatively equal amounts of happiness and suffering. An unfortunate few (at the bottom of the curve) will endure lives of extreme suffering, while a lucky few (at the top of the curve) will enjoy lives of extreme comfort. The rest of us, most of us, are somewhere in the middle.

This was the intended design of the system, according to the God in my head.

In the end, suffering and happiness are nothing more than mathematics. Whether or not there is any meaning behind the math is a separate discussion (see subchapters IV and XIV).

That said, we're back to the same question: if prayer doesn't change fate, and fate is random, is there any point in praying?

The short answer is: Yes.

As I stated previously, I believe prayer has virtuous meditative properties. It is also a noble and heart-warming sentiment to offer friends and loved ones in their hours of need.

For truly devout "believers," prayer can also work as a kind of placebo, activating the power of the mind to heal and reconfigure certain biological responses. This only works for people with a somewhat delusional level of faith. Jesus compared this kind of faith to that of children, who are willing to believe nearly anything wholeheartedly. Likewise, in the Bible, Jesus almost always prefaces his healings with the words, "*If you believe*, you will be healed."

Science is still sadly lacking in its understanding of the human brain. We know that the mind can intentionally regulate blood pressure, pain management and other bodily functions through simple meditation.[40] Through studies of the placebo effect, we know that some medical conditions can be cured simply by fooling someone into thinking they have been given a remedy.[41]

Can the power of the mind cure cancer or AIDS? Could it mend a broken bone or regrow a missing limb? I highly doubt it, but then, God never really specified the extent to which extreme faith could heal the human body. He only reiterated that He was never actually intervening in such cases, but rather the subject's own mind was capable of self-healing.

There's one other important aspect of prayer that's worth noting. God told me that no matter what kind of believer or non-believer you are, He's always listening and always sympathizing with the prayers offered to Him. He is literally divided up and scattered into all of mankind. He is with each of us every step of the way (whether we are destined to be hit by buses or not). When we pray, we are not praying to some distant God, we are, in a sense, praying to ourselves. We are praying to that tiny piece of God that dwells within us.

In the end, just before any bus runs us over, that tiny piece of God activates into something more than just a sympathetic ear, but a spirit guide (our "failsafe" mechanism). This function of God operates with or without your "belief" in Him, and with or without your use of prayer.

Overall, God left me with the impression that prayer was an overwhelmingly positive tool. He seemed to embrace all forms of prayer, from all religions, and even non-religions. The only thing prayer couldn't do, that we sometimes wish it could, is change our destinies. Destiny is what it is.

So talk to Him. He's always there, listening and holding your spiritual hand, ready to leap into action if shit really hits the fan, and ready to cheer you on as you pick yourself back up from the inevitable hard falls of life.

PART XIII: CHILDISH THINGS

Have you ever had a child draw you a picture? Even if the kid isn't your own, there's something about it that makes you want to hang it on your refrigerator. It is a phenomenon that even I, a cynical city slicker with little interest in half-pint humans, cannot resist.

Perhaps this makes me a raging narcissist (I am, after all, the guy who saw God as a mirror image of himself), but my favorite thing is when a kid draws a portrait of me. The elements of a child's drawing always seem to expose something about how the child views me in their world. The facial expression, the clothes, the actions I'm performing, how weak or how strong I appear, etc. In a way, these perceptions teach me something about myself, or at least, about how I am perceived.

Well, in my hallucination, this is how God described all of the world's religions. He said they were equivalent to pictures drawn of Him by His children. No matter how crude or how elaborate, each "drawing" had a hallowed place on God's big refrigerator in the sky. And just like when a kid draws a picture of us here on Earth, each religion teaches God something unique about Himself and about how His children perceive Him.

The analogy of the child's drawings also captures the notion that God did not "draw" any particular religion Himself. Rather, God's children, mankind, created religion as a means of capturing God's likeness.

He told me about "the age of the prophets," when a simple conversation with a mortal (like the one I was having) could spark a spiritual revolution. I asked if He interacted with the founders of various religions as transparently as He was interacting with me. He said that He did, but that humans were poor messengers of God's words. He said it was like trying to filter precise images through distorted glass.

For example, in the hands of the "ancient organizers," the difficulty of communicating with God became viewed as God's intentional separation with Man because of mankind's moral inferiority, which was untrue. If God had intended for mankind to be able to see Him clearly, without the lenses of their own minds and spirits, God would have created us that way. In reality, God created mankind perfectly and there was nothing that mankind could ever have done to make themselves somehow "imperfect." Mankind was not powerful enough to thwart God's perfection.

Every human's unique imprint on God is essential to their relationship with Him. The early religious leaders could not grasp this entirely, and so the messages they took away from their encounters with God varied drastically in their interpretation.

He explained further that while no man is spiritually blind, all men have spiritual blind spots. That is, no one is capable of holding the entirety of God's wisdom. Yet, with every passing generation, the collective mind of mankind widens and our spiritual vision increases (this is somewhat in the vein of the "collective unconscious" that Carl Jung and other philosophers and psychologists have theorized about). Humanity's understanding of the world, both physical and spiritual, grows exponentially with time. The seed of individual awareness continues to blossom into a universal awareness. It is not a simple, linear growth but a complex, winding vine that forks and coils in many directions all at once. For this reason, God said, "The roots of the old religions are strong, even as their fruits wither and are replaced every season."

This phenomenon of spiritual evolution, through gradual mutation, mimics the physical world and accounts for both the changing history of each world religion as well as the broadened theology that God was presenting to me.

He said that Moses and Isaiah and Jesus and Muhammad and Buddha and Martin Luther and Gandhi were all considered fools and liars who preached heresy in their day, yet each of their names is now carved in history alongside the other great prophets, poets and changers of mankind's destiny. Each of these men heard God's voice more fully than the last. Over and over, this cycle must continue; it is our destiny as a species.

There was one other virtue that God told me about the old religions. It was the virtue of tradition.

At first, something about the idea of honoring old rituals that meant little or nothing to me personally seemed unnecessary, if not inane. I had no real spiritual traditions of my own, only a handful of secular, American holiday traditions that were more tongue-in-cheek than anything. I knew little about the spiritual rites of my ancestors.

Then a memory bubbled to the surface.

My grandparents on my father's side were devout Catholics (Italian). My dad was named John after a distant relative (though obviously rooted to the Biblical namesake of Saint John) and after he converted to Southern Baptist in order to marry my mother in the early 70s, the indignant Catholic side of the family began calling him "John the Baptist" – half in jest and half in honest disappointment.

When I visited the Vatican on a work-study trip to Rome as a teenager, I brought back a decorative, carved-stone rosary for my grandparents. As a non-Catholic, I didn't really know what a rosary *was*. To be honest, I still don't really know. It just looks like a tiny necklace that people hold when they pray, but I'm not sure what it represents beyond that. This could easily be solved with a quick Internet search, but there's something about the mystique of it that I like. Not knowing somehow makes it more sacred, more magical.

Ever since my grandparents died, every time I pass one of those monolithic Catholic churches in Manhattan, if I have time I go inside and light a candle for them. Again, I don't know what the tradition of lighting a candle represents for Catholics, but it always feels right when I do it. Whatever it means, my grandparents understood it, and that's enough for me. In a way, it allows me to make it my own tradition, and there is something powerful about that. I light the candle in hopes that it somehow sends a message to the other side that my grandparents might hear – a message that assures them that they have not been forgotten.

This is the closest thing I have in my life to a sacred ritual. Remembering it made what God was telling me about the inherent beauty of "tradition" begin to resonate.

Before we left the subject of world religions, I asked about the dark side of such beliefs – holy wars, jihads, Hindus murdering Muslims, Christians torturing Jews, Buddhists lighting themselves on fire in the streets, sociopaths acting on "God's orders" – the list is appallingly endless.

God seemed unfazed. He simply said that "religious violence" was never about religion. Rather, it was about money, property, political power, retribution, fear, greed or simple mental disorder, all under a facade of faith. Religion merely becomes a tool of manipulation, used to raise armies and to justify violent acts. He said that men who orchestrated such abuses of faith had lost sight of whatever part of God they ever knew.

Nevertheless, such events played their part in the great history of things. Evil, in the form of misguided religion or otherwise, is all part of humanity's necessary path towards understanding the full spectrum of existence.

In the end, God seemed to believe that religion would ultimately be responsible for more good in the world than evil. Most notably, He harped on the idea that there was an unavoidable theological thread that pierced through every religion. There is a reason, He said, that all the world's religions share one perfect tenet in the core of all their teachings. The tenet is to "love others as yourself," and it appears in every major faith tradition[42] because it encompasses all you must know about God and the Universe in one perfectly articulated thought. Through God, we are all literally connected as one infinitely complex Entity, which we call "the Universe," and therefore, if anyone harms another it is equal to harming oneself.

Yet, if all of the world's religions had the same message at their core, why were they all so very different? God said religious *institutions* were products of the physical world; therefore, they were each pulled slightly away from their core spiritual tenets in order to build temples and stained glass windows and golden domes. God said this was not nefarious, but normative, healthy human behavior. Humans focus heavily on the material world by necessity, and their religions cannot help but to be swayed by this ingrained survivalist impulse. While we may applaud those who rise above these impulses, the spiritual institutions of our species are no more pure, nor wicked, than we ourselves are. In this way, religions are similar to political democracies in that they are only ever as compassionate or as cruel as the majority of the people whom they represent.

I suggested most people today were hungry for the *truth* about God, and eager to get away from meaningless or unhealthy superstitions. I certainly was. But God refuted this and told me that most people didn't want the truth; they wanted order, and they wanted validation for whatever ideas they already held. People want to feel as though the chaos of the Universe is somehow under control (either their control, or God's) and they want reassurance that they themselves are good and righteous human beings. Our need for these things is so strong that we will trample over the truth if necessary to attain them.

To help navigate through these tumultuous waters, God gave me a simple litmus test for all the world religions. He said that you can always tell what lies at the heart of a religion not by how they promise to reward their most obedient followers, but by how they promise to treat those with dissenting opinions. Any institutions that pass severe judgment upon all those who do not agree with their exact doctrines should have their true motives examined with some degree of skepticism.

God is love. The more love a religion saturates itself in, the closer to the truth it is. Therefore, let love be your guide.

PART XIV: PURPOSE DRIVEN LIFE

In ancient times, people attributed everything that they could not explain to invisible, supernatural beings – storms were caused by gods fighting in the sky, mental disorders were demon possessions, foodborne illnesses were proof that a god had cursed the food, etc. However, as humanity progressed, we slowly began to solve the natural mysteries of our planet, reducing the need for superstition. Every time an advancement was made in mathematics, biology or astronomy, the "gods" lost yet another of their divine secrets and, thereby, their powers.

Today, we have confirmed explanations for so much of the natural world that there is little mystery left for our gods. From what I can tell, there are only three obvious questions that science cannot answer. Where did it all come from? Is there any purpose to life? And is there life after death?

I've already covered the first question (in Part III) and I've implied the answers to the second and third questions, though I will clarify those answers in this section and the next (Part XV).

Obviously, you can't have a 200-year conversation with God without talking about the meaning of life. If you've been paying close attention, you already know the answer. However, I am happy to review it and spell it out explicitly.

As you know from previous sections, God created the entire Universe as a means to understand who He was, and what He was capable of. Mankind was the crown jewel of His Creation, the "Divine Species."

When God created us, we inherited His own traits of self-exploration; this is what it means to be made "in the image of God." We were designed with this function of self-discovery in mind, and as such, we were made perfect in His eyes.

Our purpose, therefore, is simple. It is to experience life. That's it.

There are no rewards for handling life better or worse, no punishments for making a mess of it all. Life is not a riddle that must be solved. There is no grand task that must be completed. There is nothing that you must do, nothing that you must avoid doing. Your only purpose is to simply exist, and here's the good news: you are already fulfilling it.

God wants you to come to know yourself, because in so doing you come to know God. This quest has no beginning and no end. You cannot stray from your path because there is no path to stray from.

For some people, this might come as a fantastic relief. For others, people like me who function best with deadlines and checklists, this answer is terrifying, if not infuriating.

Shouldn't we all be doing something? If not, why bother doing anything...ever? Why not just sit in a room and do nothing for our entire lives? Well, one could argue that monks and nuns do just that. The hardest thing for us humans to do is nothing. Most of us can't handle it. We instantly reach for our TV remotes, our iPhones, our laptops, our books. Five minutes of sitting in silence and quieting the mind is a feat that few of us have ever even attempted, let alone mastered.

Nevertheless, just because our purpose on Earth does not require any particular "doing" does not mean that there are not plenty of things worth being done. The exciting (or potentially daunting) task for each of us is that we each get to decide what is worth doing for ourselves.

The list of possibilities is endless: traveling the world, studying the arts, studying religion, growing a garden, connecting with your family, loving someone unconditionally, loving yourself unconditionally, overcoming your fears, helping others, writing a book, changing the world...whatever you want! (These are just some of the things *I* want to do before I go.)

If you need a checklist in order to make yourself feel purposeful, by all means, make a checklist! I just wouldn't let anyone else make the checklist for you, if I were you. But suit yourself! There are no rules.

All that being said, despite the fact that God has not ordained any mandatory tasks for us to actively complete here on Earth, His intention was clearly that we should find peace and happiness in our own ways while we're here. Of course, statistically speaking, some people will always walk the Earth suffering, punishing themselves, being punished by others, etc. However, His message – given to us through all of the world's various religions – was always to offer support, comfort and betterment of the human condition. His intent has always been to build us up, not tear us down. This is not to be confused with having a "purpose" of finding peace or happiness in life, but it is a worthwhile token of God's good faith and His love for mankind, despite the complexities of the free will He has given us.

As the great scientist Carl Sagan once said, "We are a way for the Cosmos to know itself."[43] So exist. And when possible, coexist with others. In so doing, you fulfill your role in helping the Universe to know itself. This is the only purpose of life.

PART XV: Happily Ever Afterlife

From previous subchapters, you know that Heaven and Hell are figures of speech relating to life on Earth. Furthermore, you know our purpose in life is merely to exist; a task at which we cannot fail, and even if we could, it would have no bearing on our status in the afterlife. So what does this all mean about life after death? *What happens when we die?*

This age-old mystery was explained in a way that was completely foreign to me. If my hallucination was purely the byproduct of my subconscious mind, I cannot tell you when or how I was ever exposed to the following ideas (unlike some of the other theological roots laced throughout this book).

It turns out that the afterlife is extremely complex, with layers upon layers of postmortem possibilities. I'm talkin' limitless space-time travel, multiple dimensions and, eventually, a paradoxical end to "eternity" itself.

The first thing you need to know is that you *do* have a soul, a spiritual consciousness that is not lost upon death. As you probably already suspect, when we die, our souls are released from our physical bodies. They are then guided to the spiritual plane by that tiny fragment of God that exists within each of us (see Part IX).

After death, the soul exists outside of space and time. In this state, you have several options at your phantom fingertips. You can linger in the vicinity of your recent life, check out your own funeral or whatever. Or you may speed off into outer space, checking out all of the celestial phenomena in the heavens. You can peek in on other time periods throughout history, either long before you were born or long after you've died. All of time and space are at your disposal.

You also have the option of reincarnation, reentering the world in any period of human history, for any reason you choose. For example, after a hectic life of being a Wall Street businessman in 2012, you may elect to teach yourself what it is to live a life of quietude, so you choose to return as a farmer or a monk in 780. Or, after living a life as a straight-laced minister in 1845, your spirit may choose to expose itself to indulgence and recklessness, reincarnating as a rock star in 1969. Stranger still, perhaps you lived a long, healthy life, dying gracefully at the age of 120, so you return as a child who dies of cancer at the age of 7, simply to know what the Universe looks like from that perspective. The possibilities are endless. I suppose you might call this "elective reincarnation."

If, on the other hand, you need a break from the earthly realm, you may elect to sit on the sidelines for a while and merely enjoy the spirit world. To me personally, this sounds heavenly (for lack of a better word). Life is fraught with trials and pitfalls; the idea of having to reenter the world over and over seems utterly exhausting. I can't imagine ever wanting to leave the spiritual plane. But then again, God told me that this was a typical reaction from someone inside an earthly life cycle. Once you're in the spirit world, however, and time is no longer measured in decades but in eons (if it's measured at all), your perspective changes.

It's a bit like when people retire too early. The rest of us think that sounds amazing, but the young retiree almost always ends up starting a new business or going back to work electively. Money may no longer be the primary incentive, but the drive to work towards a goal, collaborate with others and to achieve personal growth is too strong – to say nothing of the negative effects of sheer boredom. Likewise, most souls elect to reenter the world and continue their existential development.

Every time a soul reenters the world, they are stripped of any direct memory of their previous lives. Otherwise, their past knowledge would contaminate the authenticity of their new life experiences. And every time a spirit reincarnates, it opens a new dimension of space-time (of which there are an infinite number), allowing the spirit to experience the world anew without disrupting any preexisting timelines.

It is theoretically possible, to relive the same life more than once if you'd like. However, very few souls apparently do this, because you'd just end up making all of the same choices again, which would be kind of pointless. In fact, because the factors of genetics and environmental conditioning are so strong, most of the countless multiple dimensions that exist are virtually identical to one another. There are exceptions to that rule, but I did not press God for details. (One reality is more than enough for me to comprehend.)

I should point out that all this stuff about multiple dimensions is more of a scientific technicality than a theological point of interest. For this reason, I won't spend time discussing it further, and besides, I really have no knowledge to discuss. There are, however, many fascinating books on this subject by experts in the field of theoretical physics for those interested.

As novel as all of this sounds, none of these post-life exploits are, strictly speaking, necessary. There are some spirits who choose not to pursue them at all – neither the exploration of space-time nor reincarnation. Why not? Probably because of what's waiting for us all at the end of eternity.

No matter how many times you choose to reincarnate or how many billions of stars and planets you choose to explore on your own, the ultimate destination of the spirit world is the same. In the end, all of our souls will join together to create one unified consciousness, in what God called the "all-soul."

The all-soul is literally like a spiritual hive, a harmonious collective, made up of all of our souls and the trillions of tiny fragments of God that were previously dispersed during His "spiritual supernova" (see Part VI). That is, our souls will join together to reform God into His *original state*, creating a comprehensive, existential understanding of all life in the Universe. Every life experience will be accessible to the whole. In this state, you will be aware of your own individuality, yet simultaneously aware of the life experiences of every living organism that ever was.

In short, it will be as if each soul were a self-aware neuron within the mind of God Himself. In the all-soul, we will know the knowledge of the Universe in its entirety, because we will be a part of its consciousness.

As we've already covered, every major world religion has a core teaching to "love others as you love yourself." This is not merely a nice platitude, but because of the all-soul, it is a literal truth. At the end of time, all things will *literally* be connected as one. Therefore, you should not love your neighbor out of an aloof sense of civility; you should love your neighbor because, in the end, you *are* your neighbor. You should love your enemy because, in the end, you *are* your enemy.

At the end of things, it will be clear that whatever you did unto others, you also did unto yourself. Likewise, whatever you did to yourself, you did to the entire Universe.

All of Creation is ultimately part of one Entity, and that Entity is God (or whatever you'd like to call Him/Her/It).

God told me that I was not the first to receive this lesson from Him. Yet, many of the ancient religious thinkers interpreted these things very differently. Some faith traditions portrayed this phenomenon as Hades, Sheol, Duat, Chi, Tao and so on. Others viewed the all-soul as if it were intended as some kind of judgment, a time of reckoning between us and God or between the spirits of victims and evildoers. Those interpretations were obviously not quite accurate, but in a way, they do make sense. Every "sin" you've ever committed will be exposed to the collective. In fact, every thought and every action of your life will be documented with complete transparency. That is certainly a terrifying thought for most of us. However, God assured me that after millions of years of cosmic existence and countless reincarnations, even the most heinous of thoughts and acts become relatively trivial. Love, understanding, acceptance and forgiveness will trump everything else. In the Bible, this is what the poetic image of "the wolf lying with the lamb"[44] was meant to symbolize (often misrepresented as "the lion and the lamb," not that it matters).

When this complete picture of God finally coalesces at the end of time, the purpose of the Universe will be complete. Every piece of the Cosmos – every soul, every animal, every plant and stone and star – will merge into the collective fabric of the God-mind. Each unique identity within the all-soul will understand itself more fully when seen within the context of the whole. The Universe's quest of self-realization will, therefore, finally be complete. And so, at that moment, the Universe will end.

A quick side note: friends have occasionally gotten to this point in the book and wondered, "With all this talk about human beings and souls and Earth's place in the vast Cosmos, did God ever mention alien life on other planets? And if so, are they included in this 'all-soul'?" The answer, I'm afraid, is that He didn't explicitly mention alien life at all. (If He had, I would have included it in previous sections.) However, He didn't explicitly say that they didn't exist either. If anything, the implication was that there were very likely other species out there, strictly due to the vastness of the Universe He showed me. Statistically speaking, there must be life on other planets. Alas, I never asked Him. Nevertheless, if they do exist, then yes, they would be included in the all-soul, along with the rest of Creation.

To be clear, all of this means that the afterlife itself is not, strictly speaking, eternal. However, to the human mind, it is virtually an eternity. One hundred years is a long period of time for a human being to spend contemplating his or her own existence – and that's just one lifetime. Consider countless lifetimes (countless more if alien life is included, too!), to say nothing of the billions of years of celestial observation we may elect to witness in the afterlife. The possibilities are practically limitless.

At what point will you, personally, have experienced enough? How many perfect moments of happiness, how many tragic losses, how many enlightenments, how many riddles and solutions before you will have experienced so much as to have fully satisfied your spirit? However much time you think you'll need, that's how much time you'll be given, and more. The all-soul will not be complete until every piece of God's Creation *elects* to join the collective of their own free will, in their own time and on their own terms. The end won't be thrust upon anyone. Only when you choose to take your place in the chorus of Creation will your spirit progress to that final destination.

When this happens, after trillions of years of combined knowledge, we will consciously and collectively choose the perfect moment to breathe our last breath together. In that moment, hand in hand with God, the Universe will disperse, and it will be finished. This will be the end of eternity, a quiet and graceful finale to everything that ever was.

This is what God meant when He told me at the beginning of my vision that He was "the Alpha and the Omega," the beginning and the end.

PART XVI: THE CLOSING DOOR

There was a sudden flicker of bright, unwanted light, flashing across my sealed eyelids. Muffled voices and sounds of plastic and metal tools began echoing in my mind. I looked at God and tried to hold His gaze. I knew what was happening. I was waking up, and this grand vision was coming to an end. There was precious little time left.

I sensed myself purposefully holding my eyes shut, afraid of confronting whatever was on the other side. Every time my eyelids began to rise, another burst of light flooded my safe, dark world. There was a forceful current of awareness beginning to pull me, unwilling, towards consciousness – towards the other side.

I begged God to stave it off and to let me stay there with Him awhile longer, but He told me that He had already given me everything that I was supposed to know.

I asked him what I was supposed to do with all of this new otherworldly knowledge. What was I supposed to tell my father, the religious conservative? If everything He had told me about Christ's life and death and the Bible was true, didn't I have a responsibility to tell Christians the new Good News? Was I supposed to drop everything that I was doing in my life and become an evangelist for this new understanding of God and the Universe? This was the level of profound revelation that I felt in that moment.

Without hesitation, God told me that I was not *supposed* to do anything. If any specific revelation needed to be revealed to the entire world, God was capable of making that happen with or without me. There was nothing that I needed to do, or not do, in order to fulfill my part of the great story of things. My task was solely to be true to myself, to thoroughly be what I am, just as God is what He is. All the rest, He told me, would fall into place as it was always destined to do.

This all made perfect sense. *Of course* God didn't need me to do anything on His behalf – He was God! This lesson in ultimate humility became a true highlight of the hallucination for me. It not only kept me grounded, but also seemed to cast a challenge upon every religious institution throughout history. Any person who claims that God can only be understood by reading whatever book they alone are selling, must not truly understand or trust the power of their "God." If He is all-powerful, can He not do for Himself all that needs to be done in the Universe? At the very least, can He not speak to us directly and personally when He chooses, with or without the permission of some church or temple?

There was a constant rumbling now, all around us, as if we were in some underground bunker that was on the verge of being obliterated.

"What happens if I need to find you again?" I asked, still not wanting to leave Him.

While God had made it clear that I was not permitted to know details about my own future, He bent that rule (only slightly) in this one instance. He told me that I would not encounter Him again until my death. My deep-rooted dental phobia had triggered this divine "failsafe mechanism" in my mind, but that failsafe was typically reserved for guiding souls into the spiritual realm. He told me that I would not truly need Him again until my transition into the hereafter. At least, I wouldn't need Him enough to trigger the failsafe again.

The sounds of the outside world grew louder still. Someone was speaking to me, but I couldn't make out what they were saying. My eyes fluttered open for a moment, and once again consciousness flooded in. The outside world was beginning to merge with the timelessness of my encounter with God, like turbulent, brackish water.

I resisted and turned back.

"I thought we were outside of time," I shouted. "I don't want this to end; I'm not ready!"

"No one is ever ready," God replied. "It is time."

"Tell me one thing more," I pleaded. "Tell me anything that will help me in the years ahead."

He smiled and told me not one, but two things, there at the end of our journey.

First, He said that the entire Universe (and every dimension of it) was shaped like a giant fractal, and that it was filled with paradox. This had something to do with the perfection of mathematics and, quite frankly, I have no idea what it meant. Math is generally beyond my pay grade. However, the paradox issue made sense to me. I had learned already that whenever I was tempted to question whether God was this thing or that thing, either/or, He was almost always both. He was light and dark, love and hate, time and timelessness, all and nothing, always-will and never-was. By reiterating this here at the end, I assume He was telling me that whenever the answers seemed elusive to look for the paradox.

Secondly, He warned me that "when the door closes" I must not attempt to reopen it. He said I would be tempted to believe that the prescription drugs and alcohol I had taken were responsible for my encounter with Him, and that I would want to recreate these conditions (using these or other substances) in order to find Him again. However, this was not the case. He insisted that I had not found Him at all, but that He had found me. He rescued me at the precise moment that I needed Him to. This was how God interacted with mankind; he was not merely "summoned." Any attempt to force another interaction with Him would, therefore, be fruitless. It just doesn't work like that.

Then He grasped my hands firmly, looked directly into my eyes and told me that my story on the Earth was not yet complete; I needed to go back into the world and continue playing my part. He asked me to have faith, even in the darkest hours yet to come, and to know that He was always with me.

"Emmanuel," He said.

"God with us," I replied.

A sea of images flashed across my mind: bright beacons of white light representing the timeline of my existence, the formation of the stars and planets, Christ's death and the rise of the mighty Christian empire, love itself permeating all things, my father warning me not to touch the hotplate, the giant fractal Universe swirling into infinity, the all-soul at the end of time taking a deep inhalation as one collective spirit...

Suddenly, the rumbling of the outside world fell quiet, and God slowly vanished before me. I could smell something faint in the air around me, something crisp and refreshing, like rain and moss...

I opened my eyes.

I was not in the dentist's office at all, but in a deep forest, surrounded by giant trees covered in vines. The earth beneath me was dense with small flowers and ferns.

This was the same forest I had seen before; only then, it had been night. This was the allegorical place where the man and the woman had been lost, and found God's hands in the darkness. In the light of day, shaded by the thick canopy of trees, the forest was beautiful, the way I imagined the Earth looked long before humans.

Then, I saw a great hand wrap around the edge of a nearby tree. I recognized it as the same hand that had guided the woman back to her campfire in the night.

I crossed to the tree and peered around it.

There was a giant man, standing in a ray of bright sunlight that had somehow cracked through the canopy above.

It was only then that I realized I was not in my own body. I was not a grown man, but a boy, squinting to see the man's face towering above me, but my eyes could not adjust to the bright light all around Him.

I could only make out the outline, but I saw that He was not only a left hand and a right hand, like the man and woman had preached before, but He was complete, with two feet, two arms, two legs, a head and torso.

I reached for Him...but then a great breeze rustled the treetops above, allowing a brilliant burst of sunlight to pierce the shade, blinding me so that I covered my eyes and face. The sound of the rushing air grew stronger, and the sunlight became brighter.

As I looked away, I heard Him shout, "It is finished!"

The leaves and flowers began scattering all around me as the rumble of the forest became deafening.

The light of the room was blinding.

The craning chair beneath me felt strange and unfamiliar.

As my eyes adjusted, I turned to my left to find a middle-aged Jamaican woman staring at me with wide eyes, as if she had seen a ghost.

I began to laugh, weakly.

Everything in the dentist's office was exactly as I had left it over 150 years ago.

"Behold, The kingdom of Heaven is within you."

– Luke 17:21 (KJB)

CHAPTER 9:
THE AFTERMATH

I stumbled out of the dentist's office and into the cold, Manhattan afternoon, my mind still reeling from the trip.

For months, I had been wallowing in self-doubt, depression and cynicism, jaded by a string of business failures and defunct childhood dreams. I had come to believe that if God existed, He had failed me. If He didn't exist, then the world had failed me. Either way, I knew that I had failed myself.

But now, it was as if the darkly tinted glass had been removed. Even in the bleak winter air, there seemed to be new warmth on everything in my path. The leafless trees no longer seemed dead, but merely waited for new life in the coming spring. The tall buildings were no longer overbearing monstrosities, but symbols of mankind's progress. The throng of teenagers on the street was no longer a gang of delinquents, but a reminder of the sacredness of friendship. My world had literally taken on new color and meaning.

I felt like Ebenezer Scrooge waking up on Christmas morning. With Dickensian fervor, my instinct was to run up to every person I encountered and proclaim the joyous news that God was alive and well, and that the Universe was spinning in perfect harmony according to His precise design. I wanted mankind to share in my knowledge that no matter what, we were all safe, loved and beautifully created in the eyes of a conscious Cosmos.

Also like Scrooge, I realized almost immediately that I had to rein it in if I didn't want to be escorted off the "divine" subway car by a pair of "perfectly created" police officers.

From the reactions I was receiving in those first few minutes of returning to planet Earth, I knew the world did not particularly share my enthusiasm for my revelation.

My dentist gave me the honor of being one of the strangest patients he'd ever seen on nitrous oxide. My wife at the time, Candice, whom I had immediately called to share the good news, seemed not to care that I had just met God; she only wanted to know if I needed help getting home. All of this boggled my mind at the time. Why wasn't anyone else taking this as seriously as I was??

When the drugs finally wore off, I sent an email to my family, just to let them know what had happened. Their reactions were varied. My oldest sister, who once traveled with The Grateful Dead selling tie-dyed T-shirts in parking lots, had a reaction along the lines of, "That's pretty far out, brother." My middle sister, a borderline Atheist/Agnostic, said the email made her cry for some reason, but that she worried that she was potentially losing her like-minded Agnostic brother to some kind of religious superstition. My father didn't respond at all (which was sadly typical), but my mother, who admittedly didn't know what to make of it, confessed that my dad suspected that my vision of "God" may actually have been the Devil *in disguise*! Naturally, I only made things worse by explaining that "the Devil" was a man-made personification of God's own unsavory attributes, but that God Himself actually encompassed all of Creation, including the good, the bad, and the ugly ole Devil.

Over the months and years that followed, I couldn't help but to talk about this experience with some frequency. Anyone who got remotely close to me over these years spent some time on this subject, no doubt.

Like my family, my coworkers and friends have had a wide range of reactions as well (probably not unlike the wide range of reactions that readers are having at this very moment).

One friend sat with me for hours picking my brain about all the details he could think to ask. When I ran into him on the street a few months later, he told me that the things we had discussed had really impacted him, helping make sense of some things in his own spiritual journey that he had never been unable to reconcile before. I remember him saying, "You should write a book!"

I thought that was a terrible idea at the time. Why terrible? Probably because another friend nearly attacked me over the whole thing, basically calling my vision a narcissistic waste of time. He forbid me from ever mentioning the hallucination in his presence again (and I complied). This fellow was not a conservative religious person, as you might suspect, but rather a vehement Atheist who was incensed by the absurd notion that anyone could be on drugs, "meet God," and have the gall to draw any meaningful theology from it.

However, the bulk of people with whom I shared my vision seemed to receive the information with a grounded sense of awe and curiosity regarding the sheer complexity of the human brain. That is, the idea that somewhere in the depths of my mind, this web of spiritual and philosophical constructs had been seamlessly woven together so precisely as to actually have logical merit. I suppose it is for *these* people that I write this book.

"We're neither pure, nor wise, nor good.

We do the best we know."

— Voltaire

CHAPTER 10:
CHASING THE SHADOW OF GOD

Reluctantly, I must tell you that I could not follow God's advice. Despite the fact that He had warned me specifically not to come searching for Him again, I could not resist the temptation. For several years after the incident, I intentionally poisoned myself prior to any dental work involving nitrous oxide, in hopes of recreating my journey to God.

The quest preoccupied my mind, so much so that it virtually eliminated my dental phobia by diverting my attention so thoroughly. In a strange way, the ongoing search for God began to replace my fears with hope, which probably compounded my compulsion towards self-medication. But just as God had warned me, the trips that followed revealed nothing. I occasionally saw the swirling mix of starstuff and choppy glimpses of eternity that seem to be somewhat common to drug trips, but nothing as vivid or as clear as my dialogue with God had been.

The starkest difference between my encounter with God and all of my subsequent trips was my perception of time. In my original vision, time all but stopped completely. An indeterminable number of years seemed to pass (which I can only estimate to be approximately 150-200 years). However, my succeeding trips had the exact opposite effect on me. Forty-five minutes of dental work seemed to pass in hyper-speed. If I opened my eyes, I could actually see the dental hygienist's hands moving in cartoonish fast-motion.

During my last self-medicated attempt to reach God, I seemed to go particularly deep into my head. In that particular trip, I perceived over an hour and half of dental work as taking place over the course of approximately two to three minutes. (I don't have any theory that attempts to explain this reverse time distortion.) I opened my mind's eyes and found myself in that familiar part of my subconscious where I had previously encountered God. The black walls of a seemingly cavernous, dark, psycho-pit. Except this time, that's all it was. An empty void. God was nowhere to be found. The only sounds I heard were the echoing of my own thoughts, and the distant drilling.

However, this lack of hallucinogenic wonder is not what ultimately dissuaded me from future attempts. In my desire to find God, I had gone so deep inside myself that the staff at Dr. Fantastic's office could not get me out of it. By the time I eventually woke up, I was surrounded by five members of the staff, the dental hygienist who had been administering the nitrous oxide was in tears, and someone was shouting to the receptionist to call 911.

Luckily, Dr. Fantastic himself had rather heroically saved the day by flooding the nitrous oxide mask with pure oxygen, which brought me out of it. I was covered in water, and my face was raw from having been slapped repeatedly in an effort to wake me. I instantly knew I had taken all of this way too far, and that I needed to let go of this absurd pursuit.

The poor hygienist just grabbed me, held me tightly and kissed my forehead as she saw that I was awake. For a few minutes, she truly believed I had somehow died under her care. I felt horrible. I knew that I had caused all of this distress to this poor woman with my obsession of chasing "God" down these meaningless rabbit holes.

Much like my childhood, when my father warned me about the stovetop on the counter above, even though God warned me not to attempt to find Him again, I had to see for myself. Sure enough, both of my father figures were right in the end.

I had one glorious encounter with the Almighty, which is one more than most people seem to get in a lifetime. I had to embrace that for what it was. I would never see God again, at least not while I was alive.

After that last experiment with drug use and nitrous oxide, I was finally ready to let it go. God's work in my life had already been done; I had changed from being a cynical Agnostic to a skeptical Universalist. The needle on my faith-detector flipped 180 degrees. Despite all my doubting, I was a believer. Not necessarily because I had "proof" of anything, but because I *wanted* to believe.

I can psychologically rationalize that what I perceived as "God" may very well have been the result of years of spiritual conditioning collected from countless sources, regurgitated back to me from my subconscious mind. Yet, I choose to believe that this vision I had was something beyond the mere neurons of my brain. I choose to believe there is a God and that He spoke to me. I believe this not only because what He said made so much sense to me, but because the mystery and sacredness of faith is more powerful to me than the objective sterility of science. And so, for the first time my faith felt like a choice, rather than a mandate. In this way, it is the most genuine form of spiritual freedom that I have ever known.

I am confident in my experience now, knowing that I have gathered everything I could from it. I've relinquished the desire to find God again, knowing that He is capable enough of finding me if He thinks it's necessary. I trust His judgment. And isn't that the most powerful kind of faith there is? Learning to let go, and merely trusting your God?

"If you stumble about believability,
what are you living for?
Love is hard to believe, ask any lover.
Life is hard to believe, ask any scientist.
God is hard to believe, ask any believer.
What is your problem with hard to believe?"

— Yann Martel

CHAPTER 11:
DECONSTRUCTING LUCIDITY

This final chapter will attempt to explore some of the various theories as to what technically happened to me that day in the dentist chair. Strictly speaking, this information is not an essential part of the overall message of my memoir, but rather, a necessary epilogue for an inquisitive person like myself. These questions were important for me to explore. Now that I've had a few years to distance myself from the experience, and do a bit of research about cases similar to my own, I thought it would be worth sharing these findings with any of you who have equally scientific inclinations.

Nitrous Oxide & Prescription Drug Abuse

First of all, let's forget about the marijuana, the vodka, the painkillers, the muscle relaxers and the Xanax for a moment and just consider the effects of nitrous oxide.

When dentists use NO2, the machine administering the gas is actually pumping a mix of nitrous oxide and pure oxygen into the face mask. Pure NO2 would asphyxiate you, because your body needs oxygen to live. The typical ratio used in dentistry is about 30% nitrous oxide to 70% oxygen, with a safety feature that prevents the machine from delivering any more than 70% nitrous oxide.[45] So, effectively, the most nitrous oxide I could have been receiving that day was a 70% mix.

There are five levels of nitrous oxide's effect on the body, depending on exposure (level 1 being a mild dose, and level 5 being prolonged exposure to 100% NO2).[46]

Level 1: Drowsiness, tingling, giddiness.

Level 2: Euphoria, mild anesthetic.

Level 3: Hallucination, possible loss of consciousness.

Level 4: Coma.

Level 5: Death.[47]

Obviously, dentists all across the world are aiming for Level 2. The dosage of NO2 they administer safely accomplishes this task assuming that the patient's blood has a *normal blood-oxygen level.*

In my case, however, having heavily self-medicated before my appointment that afternoon, the oxygen level in my blood was far lower than normal. All of the drugs in my system acted to suppress my heart rate, which in turn delivered less oxygen to my brain. Marijuana actually blocks oxygen in the blood from reaching the brain[48], which further lowered my blood-oxygen level. Needless to say, when the nitrous oxide hit me, I plunged deep into Level 3.

Again, as stated in the disclaimer at the beginning of this book, please understand that this is a potentially fatal drug cocktail and I am in *no way* advocating this behavior. I am only offering this information to you for informational purposes, to better explain the biological realities that led to my hallucination.

I am thankful, in all honesty, that the consequences of my poor judgment that day were not more severe.

Psychology

You may have noticed that I peppered my psychedelic testimony with anecdotes from my past. While these memories are not absolutely necessary to understanding the underlying philosophies of the hallucination itself, I offer them as clues as to where certain themes may have originated (assuming, for the sake of argument, that they originated from within my own subconscious).

There is not time enough to go through each subchapter and dissect its potential psychological or theological roots, but I'll give you a few examples to highlight the idea.

The phrase "I Am," that God used to address Himself, is one that should be familiar to any devout Christian or Jew. It is repeated throughout the scriptures, most famously in the book of Exodus when Moses meets God on a mountaintop. In that story, Moses asks God for His name, so that he can tell his people (the Israelites) who had spoken to him. God says to Moses, "I Am Who I Am. Tell them '*I Am*' sent you."[49] I've always loved this phrase because it implies that God is so vast that no name can possibly define Him. In my hallucination, this broadened into a theology in which God could not be bound or captured by anything – not by name, not by creed, not by book or religion. This conception of God has been around for many thousands of years; it certainly did not originate with me.

Another example of preexisting intellectual constructs is the imagery I saw regarding the origins of the Universe. I titled that section "The God Particle" with some degree of tongue in cheek, because my vision was not incredibly far off from the rudimentary element famously theorized by Nobel Prize laureate Peter Higgs in 1964, a particle known as the "Higgs boson" (or "the God Particle," as it is called colloquially). I'd tell you what it is, but I still don't fully understand it myself. All I know is that it has something to do with the Big Bang and the question of why and how matter exists in the Universe. When I had my hallucination, I knew even less about this theory than I do now, but the point is that I knew that the theory existed. That alone may have been enough to spark the vision of God evolving from a tiny particle in empty space.

The theory of evolution, however, (another bit of science with clear ties to my hallucination) is one I knew a good deal about prior to my trip. In fact, in high school, I gave a report in which I argued that the theory was fatally flawed and that the theory of creation (which theorizes that God created the Universe) was a more scientifically plausible scenario. At first, my biology teacher gave me a poor grade and refused to let me present the report in class on grounds that it was simply incorrect information. My father, who had actually done most of the research, took the issue to the county's School Board, which subsequently overruled the biology teacher and forced him to allow me to give the presentation. My grade was also changed from a C- to a B, if I recall correctly. Years later, of course, I learned more about the topic and felt thoroughly embarrassed by the entire affair, especially everything I had put that poor science teacher through. (Sidenote: While writing this chapter, I actually tracked down that science teacher and wrote him a formal apology. He responded graciously and I have to say, I feel much better about it now. Thanks, God in my head!)

The point is that when God showed me how He orchestrated the evolution of the Cosmos and the origin of all the species on our planet, it may have been a logical combination of the two dueling halves of my own mind – the half that acknowledges the legitimacy of the scientific evidence supporting evolution, and the part of me that desires to believe that God created all things for divine purpose. Like many other aspects of my hallucination, the origin of the Universe was not an either/or scenario, but a harmonious duality. Both evolution and creation coexisted as complements to one another, not as opposites.

In the same way, good and evil are ultimately one force, not two. God and the Devil are two facets of one entity, not archrivals. Jesus Christ was both 100% human and 100% God. There was a definitive theme of paradox and plurality at play throughout my spiritual adventure. I can only imagine that this was my subconscious mind's attempt to build bridges between all of the opposing forces of my intellect. The evidence seems to be able to support such a theory, anyway.

When it comes to the "remixed" story of Christ's life in my hallucination, forget about it. I had studied that story inside and out as a teenager. While I had assumed I'd forgotten many of the details over time, it is theoretically possible that the information was stored deep in my brain and somehow resurfaced. Here again, my version of Jesus's life might have been a simple combination of memory and wishful thinking.

More than all of these things, so much of the Universalist philosophies presented throughout my vision could have been assembled slowly over the course of my entire life. For example, when I was a teenager, I participated in several "multicultural enrichment programs" through my school as a means of breaking through the typical social barriers of small town Southern life. In summer camps and weekend retreats, students of diverse racial and religious backgrounds were brought together to share their life experiences with one another. Through these programs I learned firsthand the universal power of human kindness that transcended race, religion and social status. While the Church introduced me to the basic principles of compassion, these secular programs brought them to life for me. There is no way of telling which principles of Judaism, Buddhism, Humanism, the Baha'i faith, Hinduism, Islam, Christian Science, Mormonism, Unitarianism, etc., I may have assimilated during my fellowship with these diverse people, and which of their tenets may have been woven into the fabric of this hallucination. If the mind is truly the informational sponge that we believe it to be, all of this data may have been brewing deep inside me without my conscious awareness of it, until the effects of the drugs brought them out.

Everything in my hallucination may have been cobbled together from all of these things, as well as the everyday exposure to friends, family, books, news articles, plays, movies, documentaries, National Public Radio...the list is infinite. I certainly could not say to you in good faith that the ideas presented to me in my vision were entirely unique or devoid of any connection to my own preexisting knowledge. There is a case to be made that even the most extreme and bizarre aspects of my hallucination – the aspects that seem to have no correlation to my past – could have been manufactured subconsciously from nonspecific psychological influences that are impossible to trace.

To be very clear, I am not advocating this view, necessarily; I'm simply not ruling it out. Like everything else in my hallucination, the truth is likely to be more complicated and less absolute than simply reducing it to its psychological components.

Divine Revelation

All that said, there are absolutely aspects of my vision for which I have little or no explanation.

Some of the details of God's story were so specific and so incredibly peculiar as to warrant supernatural consideration. For me, these things include God's explanation of the afterlife, the notion of Jesus Christ being a spiritual "supernova" resulting in tiny fragments of God living within us, the interpretation of the Book of Revelation, as well as the notion that God and the Devil are two sides of the same holy Entity.

An "all-soul" and a multidimensional Universe? God has the life cycle of a star? The Apostle Paul is the Antichrist? If these concoctions were pieced together by my own mind, I have to say, I am very impressed with myself. While I fancy myself to be a creative person, these things feel well beyond my creativity or my intellect, though perhaps I'm selling myself short. If that is the case, I wish my conscious brain were half as compelling as my subconscious brain.

It's also worth saying that before my hallucination, I could not have guessed a remotely plausible explanation as to the purpose of life. I could not have told you whether or not God existed, but would have suggested that He did not. I would have admitted absolute ignorance to any potential afterlife scenario. I would have suggested that sin did not exist, that the Bible was a dangerous book of hocus-pocus, and that drug-induced hallucinations were nothing more than the childish musings typical of weak-minded, uncreative teenagers in a pathetic attempt to find their "identity."

From my own first-person perspective, the fact that within forty-five minutes I could become a converted believer in God, armed with fascinating, intricate philosophical answers to the world's most divine quandaries, is *astounding*. It all feels too ripe with mystery and supernatural wonder to be dampened by my own skeptical nature.

Once again, I am not advocating this mystical view of these events, necessarily. I am simply not ruling it out.

Research

To be perfectly honest, I intended to reach this final chapter of my book and conclude that every person who has ever claimed to have visions of God – whether through drug hallucinations, near-death experiences or otherwise – is equally subjective and psychologically tethered to their environmental conditioning as I was. Moreover, their general insistence that their revelations about God and the Universe are "proof" that everything they saw was irrefutably real, irritated me to no end. I'm talking about the people you see on talk shows who write books with titles like *I Am a Medical Miracle: Proof That God Is An Old White Man and All Dogs Do Go To Heaven*. Gag me.

However, when I began hammering out that cynical thesis, I had to stop writing because I found myself making blanket statements about the validity (or lack thereof) of other people's drug trips and near-death experiences, even though I had never actually researched either one.

Reluctantly, I began a layman's investigation.

I started with accounts of hallucinogenic drug use, primarily because my hallucination was drug-induced. I expected to find similar accounts to compare to my own. This, however, was not the case.

I discussed the issue with friends whom I knew had dabbled in psychedelics. Many of them reported that the experiences they had on mushrooms, LSD, ecstasy or peyote ranged from mildly beneficial to life-altering. A common theme many of them seemed to have was a feeling that the Universe was connected and that everything became crystal clear at some point while they were tripping. These two themes were very similar to the overarching themes of my hallucination.

Also, some of them had visions that included periods of time feeling like they were in outer space, looking at stars and/or UFOs. This too had a correlation to certain parts of my experience.

The similarities ended there.

All of the people I casually interviewed ultimately remembered precious little of the details of any of their drug trips. What they could remember seemed to focus mostly on shapes and shadows, colors and light, and occasionally animal or humanoid figures that would appear and disappear quickly without any intelligible speech. The things they talked about the most were the *feelings* they had while they were hallucinating, rather than the details of the hallucinations themselves. Most of what they could recall regarding visual or auditory perception was vague at best.

By contrast, while there was a bit of fractal imagery in my hallucination, such things were very much on the periphery. The main thrust for me was obviously the incredibly lucid, language-based communication with "God," all of which I could recall in detail hours, days, months and years after the journey.

Additionally, there were several people who had wholly negative memories from their experimentation with hallucinogens. These people reported terrors, feeling like they were trapped in a nightmare, or, on the other extreme, they reported feeling overly happy, followed by great sadness, confusion and emptiness as the high wore off. I could not relate to any of these experiences, because mine was wholly positive.

I began to suspect that my drug trip was an abnormal one, at best.

Then a friend recommended I read some of the works of Terence McKenna, Timothy Leary, and a more contemporary author named Daniel Pinchbeck, all of whom advocated psychedelic drug use.

From these writers, it became clear that whatever my experience was, it was not closely linked with the effects of other hallucinogenic drugs (namely ayahuasca, or other DMT-based substances[50]). These books highlighted the same kinds of experiences that my friends had shared with me about their drug trips, ranging widely from hellish nightmare to euphoric enlightenment, but always through eclectic and often nonsensical visions.

For example, there are frequent accounts of mischievous "elves" or fairy-like creatures, ancient Egyptian-style man/animal hybrids, and even extraterrestrial aliens coming and going throughout people's hallucinations on these drugs.

Through all of these accounts, as well as many online videos of people describing their experiences, I found no testimony similar to my own. That is, while the creatures in other people's hallucinations occasionally invoked speech, such dialogue was rare and seemed only to occur in short, often repetitious, bursts. I found no account of any prolonged dialogue with one clearly defined entity, and nothing remotely close the degree of specificity and detail with which "God" spoke to me in my vision.

This is by no means a scientific sampling of all hallucinogenic drug experiences. The authors mentioned above are only some of the most well known in the field, essentially the tip of the iceberg on hallucinogenic research and advocacy. However, it was enough data for me to come to believe that I was barking up the wrong tree. These types of visions were simply too different from mine.

However, there were people out there who had encounters very similar to my own. Although, I did not instinctually suspect that there would be much of a correlation, I knew I needed to at least familiarize myself with their stories and the research being done in their field...

Near-Death Experiences (NDEs)

You may recall from the preface of this book that I never had any intention of writing about my experience of meeting God until I was given a copy of Todd Burpo's *Heaven Is For Real*, which chronicles the author's young son's hallucination while under surgery for appendicitis. Ironically, it was not until after my research on hallucinogenic drug experiences that I turned my attention back towards NDEs.

In *Heaven Is For Real*, Burpo implies that his son had a NDE, although none of the boy's vital organs ever actually stopped working. His appendix had ruptured, which is certainly a life-threatening emergency, but the boy was never actually near clinical death. Instead, the author merely emphasizes the emergency nature of the surgery and the parents' understandable fear of a worst-case scenario.

As valid and as moving as the story is, it is not a story about a near-death experience, but rather a story about a young boy's hallucination under anesthesia. Not entirely unlike my own.

Admittedly, it was on Burpo's book alone – which I found incredibly self-satisfying and unconvincing – that I had built my entire case against *anyone* who claimed to have encountered "God" in this way. Frankly, I believed they had all probably just encountered their own subconscious minds.

The fact that I had not used *my* experience as a means to proclaim "proof" of God in the way that Burpo had, made his claims that much more exasperating to me.

Nevertheless, I knew I needed to do more research on NDEs before making a sweeping attack based on just one book.

I began with individual accounts similar to Burpo's. I read Dr. Eden Alexander's book about his NDE, similarly (and irritatingly) titled *Proof of Heaven*,[51] as well as Dr. Mary C. Neal's *To Heaven and Back*.[52] Drs. Alexander and Neal's experiences were much closer to actual death than Burpo's (Dr. Alexander was in a coma for a week with no brain activity, and Dr. Neal was drowned and later revived), which at least gave them more credibility as legitimate near-death survivors. By and large, their testimonies were much closer to my experience than any others I had encountered thus far...but not eerily similar, either.

Both accounts seemed much more surreal and vague than the intricacies of what I had seen, and neither author had spoken to God directly in their visions.

Still, I felt like I was getting warmer. My interest was certainly piqued, but I knew I needed a larger data pool.

This led me to the famous 1975 study of near-death experiences by Dr. Raymond A. Moody, Jr., who published his findings of 150 NDEs in his book, *Life After Life*.[53] This is when a pattern began to emerge from the data.

First, no matter the circumstances of a patient's death (heart failure, brain trauma, attempted suicide, etc.), their visions all shared the same pattern of events. The differences in their stories only came from how the patients *interpreted* their experiences. For example, almost everyone in the study recalled being in a dark place, seeing a "being of light," meeting dead relatives, having flashes of memories from their past (all notions about NDEs that did not exist in American pop culture prior to Moody's book). Some interpreted the dark place as a tunnel or a void, some described the "being of light" as God or Jesus or pure energy, but again, the basic pattern of events was always the same.

Dr. Moody isolated about ten such patterns in his book, including ineffability (the inability to describe an event with words), peaceful or loving sensations, a loud rumbling or pounding noise, an out-of-body experience, and encountering a border or limit of some kind (like a line, a fence, or a body of water). Not everyone he studied experienced all ten of these events (some may only experience seven or eight elements), and the events may occur in various orders, but they represent the apparent basic structure of NDEs. My hallucination followed the same pattern of core events.

Most interestingly, *Life After Life* is the only reading material I have found that addressed a patient's nitrous oxide hallucination from the spiritual perspective. The author states that he reviewed many cases of drug-induced hallucinations and found that they were too dissimilar to NDEs because they tended to be "extremely vague," unlike real NDEs. However, he purposefully chose to highlight the nitrous oxide account in his book because it "*most closely resembles* the group of [near-death] experiences" (Dr. Moody's emphasis, not mine).[54]

Despite the fact that there were "a few points of similarity" between the nitrous oxide hallucination and NDEs, Moody concluded that nitrous oxide was not the same as a near-death experience for the following reasons. In the nitrous oxide case he studied, presumably the most extreme case he had found, the young female patient encountered a bright light, but it was "not personified" (like in most NDEs). She also had "no ineffable feelings of peace and happiness;" furthermore, she "repeatedly stresses the vagueness of her experience and it apparently had no effect on her belief in an afterlife."

Obviously, I found this alarmingly strange. If this nitrous oxide hallucination was the most extreme case Dr. Moody knew of, and it was the only known case study of its kind, why was it so different than what I experienced? My hallucination was inherently ineffable, yet not vague at all. The "being of light" I encountered *was* personified. The entire experience had a profound and lasting effect on my spiritual beliefs, as well as my belief in the afterlife – the opposite of the case Dr. Moody had referenced. So what was going on?

In the end, Dr. Moody's research had a surprising effect on my understanding of my own hallucination. It made me aware that the closest experiences on record to compare with mine were not drug hallucinations, but near-death experiences. It further validated my suspicion that drug hallucinations, including nitrous oxide hallucinations, were vague and dissimilar to what I had experienced.

What Dr. Moody's study lacked was a broad spectrum of patients from different cultural backgrounds. These 150 case studies, a relatively small sample for scientific purposes, were all Americans, which limits the variability of their near-death accounts. That is, environmental conditioning could still play a large role in what these people described. What did Buddhists and Hindus and South American tribespeople see in their NDEs?

Enter Dr. Jeffrey Long, co-founder of the Near-Death Experience Research Foundation (NDERF) and co-author of *Evidence of the Afterlife*.[55]

The book examines over 1600 case studies of NDEs from all across the globe.

Like Moody, Dr. Long uncovered the exact same pattern of distinct elements common to all NDEs. In addition to what Moody had previously identified, Long added two others: "a sense of alteration of time or space" and "encountering or learning special knowledge."

Is this getting creepy to you? Because it got creepy to me real quick.

Remarkably, Dr. Long's research of these 1600+ cases proved Dr. Moody's research correct. No matter where you came from or what god you believed in (or whether you believed in one at all) you saw the same series of events near death, and that series of events is the same as those I witnessed during my "hallucination."

Does any of this prove that there is truly life after death? No, not necessarily, but having done only layman-level research into this phenomenon, I have to say that I believe there is more evidence for the theory than against it.

The long and short of all this is that I began to question what the hell really happened to me in that dentist chair. Frankly, I began to wonder if I had somehow actually come close to death, or at least if my brain *thought* it was near death and automatically triggered some kind of chemical reaction to prepare me for the end (some kind of biological process that science cannot currently explain, perhaps).

Maybe my hallucination was a combination of *all* these theories – part drug, part psychology, part neurology, part death, part life, part wishful thinking, part God...the world may never know.

Conclusion

All I know for sure is what I saw that cold afternoon in New York. The questions of how and why I saw those things, while interesting, are somewhat irrelevant to me. I explore those questions solely because I have an inquisitive nature. The truth is, all that's really important to me is how this phenomenal experience of meeting God changed my life.

I have not been transformed into a completely new person, nor do I suddenly have all of the answers to life's many riddles. But I do have more answers than I started with. And those answers allow me to embrace myself for who and what I truly am, without judgment, guilt or longing. I can look at others who hold different views than my own with more understanding and tolerance than I could before, knowing that no matter how vast our differences are, we are cut from the same cosmic cloth. We are all part of the whole, each with our own divine place in the great story of existence.

Through these things, I have been given a faith that no one has ever possessed before me, yet one that everyone has always possessed all along.

I believe that there is something larger than all of this, larger than all of us, out there. There is meaning to this chaos, and although we are never immune to pain or misfortune, we are ultimately protected and cherished by a living Universe that wishes for us to thrive and triumph – for the better we come to know ourselves, the better the Universe comes to know *Itself*. This apparent consciousness of the Cosmos is what we sometimes call "God," and I choose to celebrate that. I choose to believe.

I suppose I am proposing a hybrid of theology here: a belief that God may actually exist, but that He dwells in our unconscious minds, gently guiding each of us to hear His voice in ways that we are most capable of listening. The messages we receive from that divine voice may be a purposeful intertwining of our own individual life experience and that of God Himself. In other words, "God" and "psychological conditioning" may not be mutually exclusive. They may work together harmoniously, by design.

If this is true, then truth itself may in fact be relative, based on how God chooses to reveal the "truth" to each of us as individuals – the intangible truths about the definition of God, the meaning of life, love, beauty and so on. The information God reveals may very well be the absolute truth for the person receiving it, even if it may not be absolute for everyone.

To put this in some kind of perspective, the "relative truth" that I am associating with God here may easily be compared to the relative truth associated with love. For example, if I fall in love with a woman whom I believe to be the most beautiful person in the world – her face, her body, her humor, her vitality, her understanding, her talents, her strengths, her weaknesses, even her mundane habits – her entire person, to me, may be a complex but absolute form of human perfection. Such passionate feelings, however, could not possibly serve as proof that anyone else ought to love the same woman in the way that I do. (In fact, I'd probably prefer they not!)

The point is that just because someone finds love does not mean that they have found love for the entire human species. Likewise, just because someone finds God does not mean that they have found God for everyone on the planet. God, like love, can only truly be discovered for oneself. This is one of the overarching messages of my divine hallucination. Perhaps it is for this reason that the Biblical author of 1 John defined God so simply, as "God is love."[56]

The key component of all these God-experiences, whether near-death, drug-induced or otherwise, seems to be love and universal connectedness. I realize that probably feels stale and perhaps obvious. It is nothing new. It is, after all, the core tenet of every major religion. It is the stuff that has fueled almost every song and poem ever written. Love is even the power that Harry Potter wields to defeat the evil Lord Voldemort.

Love is so widespread that even the great anti-theist, Christopher Hitchens, campaigned on its behalf during his last public appearance before his death in 2011. In a recorded segment for a television news program, a teenager asked Hitchens for some Atheistic advice. After recommending a few of his favorite authors, he simply advised the girl to "Remember the love bit."[57] You see, love triumphs over even the harshest of skeptics among us.

The message of human kindness is all around us, all the time, if we are willing to hear it and see it. It may seem tired or commonplace, but consider this: perhaps the reason that it comes up so often – in religious texts, in novels, in music and film, in everyday life – is not because humanity is so uncreative, but because it's simply the truth. Maybe love is all the Universe is really about. Maybe it has dominated the hearts and minds of every great artist, poet and prophet since the beginning of time for a reason, and that reason is that God Himself made it so. Maybe this is the one "absolute truth" on which we can all hang our philosophical hats. If nothing else, it's a magnificent way to view the world, and it can only make this temporal home of ours a more joyful, cooperative and beautiful place to live.

Regardless of all the fascinating things that God told me and showed me in my vision, none of it particularly matters. It is what it is, nothing more, and certainly nothing less. In the end, my hope for you reading this book is twofold. One, that whatever spiritual path you choose leads you to better yourself and to better the world around you, while being careful not to dampen, disrupt or otherwise harm anyone else who may be on a different spiritual path. And two, that you may not overly concern yourself with precisely what God told me in my head, but truly start listening to what He is telling you in yours.

.

JOSHUA STEVEN GRISETTI

ABOUT THE AUTHOR

Josh Grisetti was born in Washington D.C., grew up just outside of Roanoke, Virginia, and was raised in the Southern Baptist Church. He currently lives in Brooklyn, New York, with his dog, Cooter, neither of whom have any specific religious affiliation.

Josh is an actor by trade, working primarily in theatre and television. He has no formal training in writing, philosophy or religion. This memoir is his first book — and probably his last, as he has no further aspirations as a writer.

He still doesn't like dentists.

www.joshgrisetti.com

NOTES

Preface

[1] Burpo, Todd. *Heaven Is For Real.* Nashville: Thomas Nelson, 2010. Print.

[2] "Heaven Is for Real." *en.wikipedia.org*, Wikimedia Foundation, Inc., 05 March 2014. Web. 13 March 2014.

Chapter 3

[3] "Sedative-Hypnotic Drug." *Britannica.com.* Encyclopedia Britannica, Inc. 04 April 2013. Web. 13 March 2014.

[4] Romans 8:31

Chapter 5

[5] Bracha, H. Stefan, et al. "Posttraumatic dental-care anxiety (PTDA): Is 'dental phobia' a misnomer?" *cogprints.org.* Hawaii Dental Journal, [c. October 2006]. Web. 13 March 2014. <cogprints.org/5248/1/2006_HDJ_bracha_vega_posttraumatic_dental_anxiety.PDF>

Chapter 7

[6] John 20:29

Chapter 8

Part I

[7] Ecclesiastes 8:17

Part VII

[8] Luke 9:27

[9] Matthew 5:30

[10] Zechariah 9:9

[11] Ehrman, Bart D. *Did Jesus Exist?: The Historical Argument for Jesus of Nazareth,* Kindle Edition. (Kindle Locations 702-712). Harper Collins, Inc., March 2012. Print.

[12] 2 Corinthians 5:16 (ISV)

Part IX

[13] Franklin, Joseph C. "How Pain Can Make You Feel Better." *scientificamerican.com.* Scientific American. 16 November 2010. Web. 13 March 2014.

[14] European College of Neuropsychopharmacology. "How Does the Opioid System Control Pain, Reward and Addictive Behavior." *sciencedaily.com*. ScienceDaily, 15 October 2007. Web. 13 March 2014.
[15] Seligson, Susan. "Cutting: The Self-Injury Puzzle." *bu.edu*. Boston University, 3 April 2013. Web. 13 March 2014.

Part X
[16] "Adam." *en.wikipedia.org*, Wikimedia Foundation, Inc., 11 March 2014. Web. 13 March 2014.
[17] "Eve." *en.wikipedia.org*, Wikimedia Foundation, Inc., 18 February 2014. Web. 13 March 2014.
[18] Leviticus 20:9
[19] Leviticus 20:13
[20] Leviticus 20:18
[21] Isaiah 6:2
[22] Daniel 10:5-6
[23] Ezekiel 10:9-14
[24] 2 Corinthians 4:4
[25] Matthew 6:9-11
[26] Revelation 17:7
[27] Revelation 3:8
[28] Romans 9:20-23
[29] Revelation 13:11
[30] Revelation 13:12
[31] Revelation 13:7

Part XI
[32] Strauss, Lehman. "The Doctrine of Sin." *Bible.org*. Bible.org. 25 May 2004. Web. 13 March 2014.
[33] "Greek and Hebrew words for Sin." *Theopedia.org*, N.p., N.d. Web. 13 March 2014.
<http://www.theopedia.com/Greek_and_Hebrew_words_for_Sin>
[34] Miller, Dave. "The Age of Accountability." *apologeticspress.org*. Apologetics Press, [c. 2003], Web. 13 March 2014.
[35] Matthew 22:36-40

Part XII
[36] "Lottie Moon." *en.wikipedia.org*, Wikimedia Foundation, Inc., 07 March 2014. Web. 13 March 2014.
[37] Philippians 4:19
[38] Psalm 147:5
[39] Malachi 3:6

[40] University of Kentucky. "Meditation Can Lower Blood Pressure, Study Shows." *sciencedaily.com*. ScienceDaily, 15 March 2008. Web. 13 March 2014.
[41] Knox, Richard. "Half Of A Drug's Power Comes From Thinking It Will Work." *npr.org*. NPR, 10 January 2014. Web. 13 March 2014.

Part XIII
[42] "Golden Rule." *en.wikipedia.org*, Wikimedia Foundation, Inc., 10 March 2014. Web. 13 March 2014.

Part XIV
[43] Sagan, Carl. "The Shores of the Cosmic Ocean." *Cosmos: A Personal Voyage*. Public Broadcasting Service, 28 September 1980. TV.

Part XV
[44] Isaiah 11:6

Chapter 11
[45] Austin, Mary Lou. "Nitrous Oxide Sedation: Clinical Review & Workplace Safety." *dentallearning.org*. The Academy of Dental Learning & OSHA Training. [c. March 2013]. Web. 13 March 2014.
[46] "Inhalation Sedation (Laughing Gas)." *dentalfearcentral.org*, Dental Fear Central, N.d. Web. 13 March 2014.
[47] "Nitrous oxide fact sheet." *cganet.com*. Compressed Gas Association, N.d. Web. 13 March 2014. <http://www.cganet.com/n20guidelines.php>
[48] Davis, Katherine. "Marijuana makes blood rush to the head." *newscientist.com* [reference *Neurology* (vol. 64, p 488)]. Reed Business Information Ltd. 07 February 2005. Web. 13 March 2014.
[49] Exodus 3:14
[50] *DMT: The Spirit Molecule*. Dir. Mitch Schultz. 2010. Gravitas Ventures, 2011. DVD.
[51] Alexander, Eben. *Proof of Heaven*. New York: Simon & Schuster, 2012. Print.
[52] Neal, Mary C. *To Heaven and Back*. 2011. Colorado Springs: Waterbrook Press, 2012. Print.
[53] Moody, Raymond A., Jr. *Life After Life*. 1975. Bantam Books, 1976. Print.
[54] *Life After Life*, pg. 158-160. (see above)
[55] Long, Jeffrey, with Paul Perry. *Evidence of the Afterlife: The Science of Near-Death Experiences*. 2010. [Unabridged] Audible audio ed. HarperCollins, 2011. Audio.
[56] 1 John 4:8

[57] Hitchens, Christopher. "Fighting Faith." *Dateline*. SBS. Houston: 30 October 2011. Television.

Made in the USA
Middletown, DE
29 December 2018